WOMEN WHO MADE MONEY

Women partners in British Private Banks

1752–1906

By Margaret Dawes and Nesta Selwyn

Order this book online at www.trafford.com
or email orders@trafford.com

Most Trafford titles are also available at major online book retailers.

Printed in the United States of America.

ISBN: 978-1-4269-3725-5 (sc)
ISBN: 978-1-4269-3726-2 (hc)

Library of Congress Control Number: 2010912411

Trafford rev. 11/05/2010

 www.trafford.com

North America & international
toll-free: 1 888 232 4444 (USA & Canada)
phone: 250 383 6864 ♦ fax: 812 355 4082

FOREWORD

This is not a usual kind of book about banking or bankers. In the financial crisis of 2007–09, the business which underpins our assumptions about life in an advanced social and economic system came perilously close to collapse, with unimaginable consequences for most of us. So this book comes at a time of unparalleled interest in banking, and of public bafflement and outrage at the spectacular failings of banks – and the cost to taxpayers of attempts to repair the damage. As the book shows, however, there may be nothing new in all this apart from the sheer gigantic scale of the most recent problems.

The accounts of women described here, all prominent in their banks of the 18th and 19th centuries, show hard work and commitment, successes and failures. What they had in common was a level of responsibility as partners in banks which was far in advance of their legally-recognised rights in financial matters. So inevitably the women who undertook such responsibilities were people of remarkable character, and we meet plenty of them in the course of this book. There is the well-connected, seemingly irresistible and immensely rich Harriot Coutts, and Elizabeth Evans of Derby who promised to be *'diligent, temperate and virtuous'*, and who became in the words of Coleridge *'the greatest woman I have been fortunate enough to meet with.'* As to Catherine Marsh, *'humble in prosperity, cheerful in adversity ..... and abounding in charity'* whose Reading bank went down in 1815, her virtues would not have come amiss in leaders of more recent and much greater bank failures.

Responsibility as partners in banks did not absolve many of these characters from the more usual concerns and obligations of women at the time. So we hear in the book about domestic matters – childbirth, sickness, dinner services, furniture, watercolour painting and riding accidents. There is also a background of links with commerce and business which made the British economy so vibrant and dynamic at this formative time. Agriculture was still of fundamental importance, but the banking industry grew and developed in response to the needs of enterprise in shipping, textile manufacture, mining, engineering and general commerce.

In all this, close local relationships were the core of the business, and some inevitably went wrong. A bank in Kettering went bust as a result of a hefty unsecured loan of £46,000 to the Rev. Macpherson (although it must be said that this imprudent decision was made after the retirement of the bank's female partner). Personal privation and hardship were suffered by bank partners and their families as a result of such failures before the days of limited liability. But equally there were instances of banks being rescued by the support of customers when times got hard.

The banks and bankers described were rooted in local communities and enterprises in ways which weakened as banking became the preserve of giant international corporations. Whatever conclusions might be drawn about the effectiveness of these women bankers in times of closer connection with the real world around them, here is a book full of banking history and characters. It is mercifully light on references to subprime lending, liquidity ratios, securitisation, or even bonuses. This is an excellent time for it.

Adam Butcher, Oxford 2010

Acknowledgements

The core information given by many librarians and local historians I gratefully acknowledged in the list of references under each banker. Many other people, including family and friends, have given us interesting details, for which our sincere thanks. These include W L Banks for his kindness in inviting Nesta Selwyn and me to visit the house in which the banker Esther Crummer once lived and for allowing us to use the notable family archive. Also to Dr Roy Fenn, archivist, who gave Nesta and me so much detailed information, and Dr John Ross who photographed her portrait.

I warmly acknowledge the kindness of those who have given me personal information about bankers who were members of their families as well as those who dug into local records. Among these are Majorie Betton, Elizabeth Deighton, Ann Denier, R M Fitzmaurice, R A Gunner, Dr Michael Haggie, Margaret Hammond, E B McLellan, Brian Rice, Henry and Ann Rice, and J L S Whitney.

Adam Butcher's kindness in reading and commenting on the text is most gratefully acknowledged. We thank him most warmly too for his further kindness in writing the Foreword. Zoë Spilman for her work in obtaining the illustrations. Alison Bickmore has helped in so many ways, including assisting with mathmatics and in solving computer problems, for which very many heartfelt thanks. I want warmly to thank Jackie Finlay for her kindness and skill in managing the drafting and preparation of the text for publication, liaising with publishers and helping with the practical problems. Her friendship has made these tasks a pleasure. We gratefully thank Keith Bennett for his very considerable assistance in our final preparation of the book.

Lastly, warm thanks to my family for continuing help and support and especially to my sons Nicholas and Martin and my grandson Christopher for constructing and maintaining the computer programme with voice synthesizer which enables me to work.

Contents

Foreword v

Acknowledgements...vii

Preface xi

Introduction..xiii

Chapter One. Independent Wives. 1

Chapter Two. Founders and Opening Partnerships 17

Chapter Three. Wives in partnership with their husbands.................29

Chapter Four. Women in partnership with other relatives.................35

Chapter Five. Widows inheriting banks from their husbands............55

Chapter Six. Widows inheriting banks from their husbands.............79

Chapter Seven. Widows inheriting banks from their husbands
(Cheshire and Yorkshire) 93

Chapter Eight. Widows inheriting banks from their husbands
(Midlands and Wales)...101

Chapter Nine. Widows inheriting banks from their husbands 123

Conclusions..139

References 151

Table Indicating the fates of the women bankers 167

Index of women bankers and the chapters in which they appear....171

Preface

During my work on Country Bank Partnerships (*Country Banks; Private provincial banks in England and Wales 1688 to 1953* published by the Chartered Institute of Financial Services, 2000) sixty-six women country bankers were identified. Not every directory made it possible to identify women partners. The main source for *Country Banks*, the annual Post Office Directories, list only surnames. Leekey includes forenames in lists of application to issue notes in 1814. They are also given in Twigg's *List of Country Bankers* of 1830. Nesta Selwyn and I made use of published works and many personal communications quoting primary sources. The kindness of these correspondents is gratefully acknowledged elsewhere.

We have subsequently identified a total of seventy-one women partners in fifty-eight country banks. Five women, in three London banks are already in the literature making up the total of the seventy-six women discussed here. Nesta Selwyn and I were amazed to find that so many women at such an early date had taken upon themselves the responsibilities of banking, which stimulated us to delve more deeply into their personalities. We were fascinated by the wide variety of women who had involved themselves in these partnerships and were encouraged to continue our research into their lives.

The names of the banks in which the women were partners perhaps need an explanation. The Alexanders, for instance, were partners in Alexander & Co. This stands for co-partnership and not company. When legislation allowed country banks to form themselves into limited liability companies the bank name ends in Co meaning a limited company.

A brief biography of each woman banker is given, showing her in the context of her family and her community as well as the background history of the bank in which she was a partner.

Each chapter represents the way in which women entered partnership, as a founder, or joining a relative or being bequeathed the bank on the death of her husband or other relative. The bankers in each chapter are discussed in chronological order of their entry into the bank. The name of the town is listed at the beginning of the biography of the partner. The largest group, widows inheriting the bank from their husbands, described in Chapters 5 to 9, are divided geographically, emphasizing aggregations such as that in the south-west. Within these divisions the partners are described chronologically, as in earlier chapters.

Margaret Dawes
Oxford 2010

Introduction

Women still do not find it easy to combine holding down a job with running a home and family. It is difficult to imagine the courage and determination a woman needed in the eighteenth and nineteenth centuries to do all these things. There were periods when gross belittlement of woman's intelligence went unchallenged. *'Girls'* one fictional pedagogue asserted *'can pick up a little of everything ….. they've a great deal of superficial cleverness, but they couldn't go far into anything. They're quick and shallow.'* Thus, in the *Mill on the Floss*, Tom Tulliver's tutor blandly told him, to explain how his clever little sister Maggie managed to do better at his lessons than he could. George Eliot, while feelingly demonstrating how a girl could be made ashamed of her own intelligence, makes clear that the tutor's view would be endorsed by most male readers of this story in 1860. The lack of education and careers available to a woman was only too well understood by other authors. Jane Austen, trying earlier in the century to achieve some independence through her writing, refers in *Emma* to the miseries of the 'governess trade.' She has her Charlotte Lucas in *Pride and Prejudice* unromantically accept that for a gentlewoman *'marriage must be her pleasantest preservative from want.'* In such a climate of opinion educated women who were prepared to use their management skills outside the home to earn their own living or contribute to the family income were exceptional.

It had, of course, always been accepted that women hampered by neither education nor social standing should trade successfully in local markets in the products of their dairies and hen-runs selling cheese, butter and eggs. In the nineteenth century pages of the London Gazette women are found in less domestic trades, such as mercers or drapers. Sometimes, perhaps, such occupations were the result of widowhood as happened in the Newcastle firm of shippers and rope makers of which Mrs Robert Hood Haggie, whose signature confirms the accounts, took charge on the death of her husband.

Traditionally, women have been in charge of savings in the home, receiving an allocation of money from which to keep the household while making what savings she can manage. Amplifying this task women have sometimes tried to help their neighbours by operating co-operative savings schemes by means of which a woman could make small regular deposits in order to buy a larger purchase than usual. Often the 'banker' would be present at the purchase to ensure that the savings were not appropriated by the male partner; such systems arising in many developing countries.

The women considered here entered private partnership banks with unlimited liability. Partners were liable for the debts of the partnership to the whole extent of their fortune, in landed property as well as money. For women with children, this must have been especially daunting, knowing that failure would lose even the roof over their heads.

From the late seventeenth century bank partnerships traded in London and in country towns in England and Wales. In the former, banks most often grew from the trade of goldsmith, while in the country much greater diversity was found. Local squires, interested in increasing the wealth of the neighbourhood, perhaps to make it easier for their agents to collect the tenants' rents, formed the largest group among the first country bankers. Traders, often representing the most important trade of the town, also made money from the new enterprise, holding their customers' spare monies in safe keeping along with their own stock.

London exerted its influence on provincial bank trading. Good communications with London was important to country towns. By 1790 eighty per cent of country banks were set up in staging post towns along the turnpike roads, with their faster and safer travel. The system of post horses, at first available only to government use, was opened to the public in 1685. This proved a strong incentive to provincial enterprise and was rapidly followed by the first country banks. Thomas Smith, a mercer of Nottingham, is credited with being the first, in 1688, to add banking to his other enterprises.

The Industrial Revolution brought new groups such as mine owners, mill owners and steel founders into banking. The number of banks rose rapidly to a peak in 1812. In their early days, provincial banking partnerships could only end in closure without loss to the public or in failure. After 1826 when legislation allowed limited liability (joint stock) companies to operate banks outside London, a third ending became available. Private partnerships could then choose to merge with or form new joint stock banking companies. Though the latter increased rapidly, private partnership banks continued to flourish, many country people preferring still to entrust their affairs to old friends rather than the new companies.

Private banks continued to adapt to new methods of communication, using the expansion of the railways to good effect. So many new branches were opened that the number of private banking outlets, taking head offices and branches together, actually increased between 1840 and 1880. Once joint stock banking had begun, it might have been expected to replace the private banking system rapidly, however, the last private country bank did not disappear until amalgamation with Barclays Bank in 1953.

The country bankers made an especially useful contribution to the national economy. During the latter part of the eighteenth century, as the economy grew, the lack of an efficient circulating currency brought problems. In spite of legislation, coins were constantly clipped for the metal, lowering their value and small denominations were hoarded, continually reducing the general supply. The issue of promissory notes, payable on demand, by country banks, and other businesses offered a solution. Their applications for a licence to issue notes are listed by Leekey in 1812 and 1813. Each country bank had their London agent, who would exchange their notes and were relied on to help with a needed loan. Partners who issued notes knew themselves to be vulnerable to a sudden demand for the exchange of large numbers of them for gold, known and dreaded as a 'run on the bank.' It could be caused by genuine anxiety or engineered through the machinations of a rival partnership or other ill wisher. Country bankers countered the real or bogus panics with some ingenuity. One put gold coins into a hot oven before shovelling them onto the counter when clients demanded the withdrawal of their deposits in gold. Exclamations over burnt fingers brought the apology that the coins came straight from the Mint. If not believed, the answer was at least regarded as a reassuring joke, illustrating confidence.

An attempt to ruin a solid Quaker banker, Jonathan Backhouse was made, from personal dislike, by the local landowner, the Earl of Darlington. He instructed his agent to collect all his rents in Backhouse's notes planning to present them all at once for payment in gold and break the bank. As soon as he learned of the plot the banker set off literally post-haste for London to obtain a loan from his agent there for sufficient gold to cover his outstanding note issue. As the post-chase neared home on the return journey a wheel flew off but Backhouse refused to stop. With his own not inconsiderable weight and the gold in one corner, the journey was completed on the remaining wheel, in time for the opening of the bank. When the Earl's agent presented himself with his bundle of notes Backhouse cheerfully told him that there was enough gold to pay all, adding *'and to buy Raby Castle if thy master will sell it.'* A cartoon of the period shows the banker in a corner of the one wheel chaise, with the caption *'Balancing the Books.'* The episode probably did not greatly endear the banker to Lord Darlington. Such imaginative counter-measures, however, could not avail in times of real economic uncertainty.

Country bankers, whether or not they issued notes were vulnerable to economic down-turns and thirty per cent of all country banks failed. Every failure caused great distress in the neighbourhood, which ensured a reputation for instability. Because of each partners' unlimited liability, every failure also entailed personal disaster. Banking, especially in the provinces, at this time was not a career for faint hearts and it is the more gratifying to find even this small number of women taking it on.

Over all but the last few years during which women held bank partnerships, a married woman could own nothing, for even her current earnings belonged to her husband. In 1870 Parliament improved her lot in so far as it now became possible for a married woman to retain annually £200 of her earnings. Only in 1884 did the passage of the Married Woman's Property Act finally enable a married woman to enjoy the same rights as an unmarried one; after that date she was at last able to carry on her trade or business using her own money.

The women bankers have not yet received due recognition and it is hoped that this account may go some way to setting the record straight.

Chapter One

Independent Wives

SARAH CHILD, SARAH SOPHIA FANE, HARRIOT COUTTS

The most audacious women bankers carried on partnerships from which their husbands were excluded, in spite of the laws debarring her from owning property, which constitutes the greatest obstacle to a married woman engaging in business on her own account.

The law has always offered loop-holes. Provision could be made in her marriage settlement for a woman to retain the use of her own property. Harriot Mellon's prudent management of her savings before marriage so impressed Thomas Coutts, the banker, that he made just such a settlement on her when they were married.

It was also possible for a woman's property to be placed in the hands of trustees before her marriage, so that her husband could have no use of it without her consent. Elizabeth Patton, banker at Chester, left her money to her daughter to be placed in the hands of trustees so that it could not be used by her son-in-law who was much encumbered by debt. The trustees she appointed were in fact related to her son-in-law, indicating that it was not a specific but a general wish to safeguard the bequest. A Hastings banker, Leonora Tilden Samson, expressed her feelings strongly in her will by only leaving £100 to her late husband's brother, but a meticulously worded bequest to her sister-in-law, his wife Mary, which states that the interest on the bulk of her estate was to go to Mary '*for her sole and disparate use.*' This was to be independent of any debts or contracts of her present husband or any future husband. The will further states that Mary was to have the money whether '*sole*

1

or couverte,' that is to say, whether single or married. The confidence felt by these women bankers in the ability of women to manage money is clear enough.

SARAH CHILD

The first of these independent wives was Sarah Child. Robert Child, no doubt mindful of his mother Agatha's successful career in banking, (*see Chapter 5*) left the senior partnership to his wife Sarah on his death in July 1782.

Sarah carried on the bank of Francis Child Esq & Co until her death in 1793. She had married Matthew Ducie, 2nd Baron Tortworth, in 1791 but never included him in her partnership. Lord Ducie's estate in Gloucestershire was known for the Tortworth Chestnut, believed to have grown from a nut planted around 800 AD, in the reign of King Egbert. Sarah and her first husband, Robert Child, had one daughter, Sarah Anne, born 26 August 1764 and died 1793. She had shown her own brand of independence by eloping in May of 1782 to Gretna Green with John Fane, 10th Earl of Westmorland, a neighbour in Berkeley Square, nicknamed 'Rapid' and heartily disliked by her father.

Robert pursued his daughter and her seducer along the road to Scotland until one of his carriage horses was shot by the Earl's postillion, and the couple escaped, a story much quoted and often with embellishments. This was scarcely a circumstance likely to reconcile Robert to his new son-in-law. He never forgave the couple but before he died in July of that same year, did give his legal consent to the marriage.

Sarah Anne and her husband had one son and four daughters. Robert, in spite of his consent, was determined that his property should not go to the eldest son, who would inherit the title and the hated name. Not wanting it to go outside the family however, he entailed his fortune and his bank, after the death of his wife, to his daughter's second son or her eldest daughter.

SARAH SOPHIA FANE

As no second son was born, the eldest daughter, Sarah Sophia Fane, became at the age of eight, when her grandmother died in 1793 an heiress and the owner of Child's bank.

Sources differ about the date of her partnership in the bank, one listing her as senior partner in 1795, when she was only ten. Another, more reasonably, gives 1806, when Sarah Sophia reached her majority, as the date when she became senior partner. However that may be, she continued in this position until her death in 1867.

In 1804 she married George Villiers, 5th Earl of Jersey, who in 1812 assumed additionally the name of Child. The couple had four sons and three daughters. With such dominant women among her ancestors, one cannot wonder that even while producing this very respectable sized family, Lady Jersey never admitted her husband into the bank partnership, but proved herself to be a most redoubtable banker. Historians differ on the role played by Sarah Sophia. One commentator did not find it easy to accept a woman in so responsible a position and suggested a frivolous approach, even putting forward the idea that the Countess of Jersey merely went to the bank parlours to read magazines. Other commentators describe her as taking a keen interest in the bank, inspecting the books, deciding who has to receive an increase, or decrease, in salary. Such involvement of course led to resentment on occasion. An instance is the argument, which ran for ten years, concerning her wish to reinstate her cousin Vere Fane in the partnership. The existing partners, she stated, had allowed a fraud of £25,000 to be committed by a junior clerk. The other partners, nevertheless, wished to continue the practice of promoting clerks to partnership in order of seniority of service rather than introducing outsiders. Some observers found that the influence of women on business ethics showed that '*the ideal of service was not for men alone*,' a generalization not altogether appreciated by Lady Jersey's partners. In their eyes, she was intent on disturbing the established pattern of running the firm and ensuring its continuity.

The argument ended in a compromise. Vere Fane never became a partner but Lady Jersey acquired the right of dismissal of any partner. Child's bank continued to flourish, undeterred by this provision, and on Lady Jersey's death in 1867 she left her grandson, Albert George Child Villiers, 7th Earl of Jersey, a partnership. She had clearly arranged to keep her separate representation even after her death, for in 1888 partners are listed in two groups, as '*representatives of Sarah Sophia, Countess of Jersey, deceased, the Earl of Jersey and Frederick William Price*,' and then again Frederick William Price, with '*Charles Thorold Fane, Frederick George Hilton Price and George Lionel Dashwood.*'

The challenges of business may well have been seen to a woman like Sarah Sophia as a welcome escape from the limitations of social life, so frustrating to an independent minded woman, but to which, without the bank partnership, she would have been restricted. Child's bank flourished for many years after her death, being sold in 1924, to pay death duties, to Glyn, Mills Banking Company. This bank was acquired by the Royal Bank of Scotland in 1939. Child & Co continued to trade under its own name as an office of the Royal Bank and later re-established its private banking tradition under the old Marygold trade sign. The Royal Bank of Scotland itself came close to collapse in the major banking crisis of 2008-2009, and had to be rescued by massive government intervention. As a result of this RBS was effectively owned to a very large extent by the British taxpayer at the time that this book went to press in 2010.

HARRIOT COUTTS

The history of the woman who became Mrs Thomas Coutts and later the Duchess of St Albans does not exactly resemble the stereotype of a staid banker. She could not have foretold in her childhood, the eminence which she would eventually achieve. Among a number of references to Harriot's mother Sarah, several varied accounts have been found. They all contain a reference to Sarah as a beautiful Irish peasant girl from Cork. She is variously described as a cotter's daughter, a shop-girl in her native city, a milliner, and a wardrobe mistress as her application to some travelling players to work did not prosper because she could not read nor write. From various sources she claims to have married Matthew Mellon, an officer in the Madras Native Infantry who deserted her two months after they were married on the '12th' day (i.e. 6 January) 1777 and that Harriot was born on 11 November the same year. It was even hinted that Lieut. Mellon was *'a person of high rank.'* An alternative version states that Mellon died of consumption on an East Indian ship between the Cape and Madras. As no Lieutenant Matthew Mellon has been found in Dodwell, Miles' Indian army list among the officers of the Madras Native Infantry between 1760 and 1834, his part in the romantic history has not been substantiated.

Harriot's mother married in 1782 Thomas Entwisle, younger than herself and devoted to her five-year-old daughter. Thomas was a violinist, working with the Thomas Bibby Players in which his wife was wardrobe mistress. The company was based at Ulverstone in the Lake District where Harriot made her first stage appearance, not yet quite ten years old, on 16 October 1787 in *Little Pickle or The Spoiled Child*. This play became a favourite at Drury Lane, where in March 1790 Dora Jordan played the role of the Spoiled Child to full houses. The play is a farce, but with no sexual overtones, and was much enjoyed by the Duke of Clarence, who began paying his attentions to Mrs Jordan a few months later.

Harriot went to Miss Calvert's day school and made stage appearances in at least eleven Midland towns. In Burton-on-Trent she met a prosperous business family who introduced her to John Wright, a Stafford banker. He, with his connection with the London bank of Wright & Co was to become an important figure in Harriot's career.

She and her family moved to Stafford in 1789 where she joined a better theatrical company, Stanton's, earning a guinea a week. The Wright family were extremely kind to Harriot, the daughters lending her their dresses and jewels. Their friendship was the more important to Harriot as her mother consistently maltreated her, flying into rages, beating her and locking her in a dark room. On one occasion Harriot ran away, missing a performance, but returned penitently the next day to her employers, the Stantons, who received her sympathetically, condemning her mother's cruelty.

John Wright introduced Harriot to Richard Sheridan, who had been Member of Parliament for Stafford since 1780. The cost of his first election was around £2,000, some of the money being raised by his offering a share in the profits of the Drury Lane theatre, of which he owned half the management. Contact between the playwright and the banker may well have come about through the need to raise the election expenses. Sheridan was taken with John Wright's protégée, but when Wright asked him to invite her to join his Drury Lane Theatre Company, he was evasive, writing to say that he would think about it.

Despite this lack of encouragement, in 1794, aged 17, Harriot took the £50 from her benefit performance and set off for London with her parents. They rented rooms in New Street, near Surrey Zoo Gardens, three miles from Drury Lane, but after three months moved to 17 Little Russell Street to be nearer the theatre where Harriot hoped to be employed. Sheridan at first pretended he had never heard of her, but her mother, unabashed, produced his letter to Mr Wright, whereupon she was told that since the season was nearly over her daughter would have to wait until the following year. Harriot's first appearance at Drury Lane was some date between January 1795 and June 1796, but certainly at the end of the 1796 Drury Lane season Harriot went to the Liverpool Theatre where she appeared in many productions.

Mrs Siddons also finished the 1796 season in Liverpool, where she befriended Harriot, of whose propriety of behaviour she greatly approved. On their return to London Mrs Siddons invited her to the Drury Lane green room, usually reserved for stars. Harriot clearly understood the importance of preserving her respectability. Had Sheridan himself not said of acting, *'for a girl (is) the unblushing object of a licentious gaping crowd . . . What is the modesty of any woman whose trade it is eternally to represent all the different modifications of love before a mixed assembly of rakes, whores, lords and blackguards, and . . . to be haul'd about, squeez'd and kiss'd by beastly pimping actors. What is to be the fate of a girl of seventeen in such a situation?'*

The good sense of combining respectability with a career on the stage must have been even more obvious to Harriot when she became a favourite of Mrs Jordan, who used her as one of her understudies during the brief periods when the birth of another of the King's many love-children made her leave the stage. The vitriolic nature of the criticism and cartoons aimed at Mrs Jordan must have strengthened Harriot's resolve to conform to the conventions, such as they were, of the times. Though not regarded as so good an actress as Mrs Jordan, Harriot was a great favourite with the public, being described as *'a handsome brunette, inclined to portliness, but with great vivacity.'* She was also considered as *'generous, ostentatious and somewhat fiery in temperament.'*

In 1798 Sheridan introduced Harriot to Mr Graham, a Bow Street magistrate, who took her to visit his cousin Sir Henry Tempest who was building a new house, Holly Lodge, at Highgate. Harriot loved its countrified freshness and was a frequent visitor. The Graham's orphaned niece, Eleanor Goddard, became a great friend to Harriot and eventually her companion for nineteen years, 1812 to 1831.

A budding romance with a Mr Barry, recently returned from the West Indies, ended in 1804 when Harriot found he was lying about his wealth. Mrs Entwisle had made every effort to thwart Mr Barry and relations with her daughter had become even more strained. Next year the Entwisles left London and opened a music shop in Cheltenham. In spite of the disagreement, Harriot bought them a house there, while she remained in Little Russell Street with a female companion. Harriot made a great pet of her, buying her dresses exactly like her own, so that they were frequently taken for sisters. Together they visited the Entwisles for the 1805 Cheltenham season, where Harriot was booked to appear at the theatre. There she met an equerry to the Prince of Wales, whom she persuaded to obtain for her step-father the office of Post Master of Cheltenham. Harriot's mother, hearing that Thomas Coutts, the London banker, was in Cheltenham, wrote to him asking him to take a box for her daughter's benefit night, a presumption to which he did not reply. However when he met Harriot whom he had often 'admired' at Drury Lane taking the air with her friend in the Long Walk he apologised for not having answered, and sent five golden guineas to her benefit fund, which she always kept for good luck.

Whilst acting at Drury Lane Harriot accumulated a comfortable bank balance with Wright & Co, in Covent Garden, connections of her Stafford banker friend. Thomas Coutts frequently visited the Drury Lane green room, though no doubt not expecting to find the prudence in business, so admired by a Scot, in a handsome young actress. He no doubt recalled that when he had met Harriot out walking in Cheltenham she had been prudently accompanied by a companion. He was soon giving her fatherly advice on the management of her finances. He counselled her to make over her fortune to trustees and, if she married, to secure it to herself by contract. From November 1805 he gave her an allowance and encouraged her to continue banking at Wrights, rather than with his own bank, perhaps wishing to conceal the allowance from his partners. He also took an interest in her personal affairs, trying to prevent her from being exploited by her mother, for Mrs Entwisle was constantly demanding money from her daughter. When Mr Entwisle was about to lose his position in the Cheltenham Post Office for lying about the arrival of an important letter, Thomas Coutts intervened to save him, though making it clear that he would not help again.

By 1807 the banker had become infatuated with Harriot. He called often in Little Russell Street though always extremely scrupulous about the respectability of his visits. Thomas let it be supposed that Harriot was his natural daughter, a perfectly acceptable supposition at that date. Nevertheless, when Harriot appeared on the stage wearing a paste necklace she was accused of flaunting diamonds given to her by her protector. She was so angry at this that she gave the necklace away. By 1808 Harriot's careful management of her money enabled her to fulfil her ambition to buy Holly Lodge, the house at Highgate that she had loved since visiting the Tempests there when she first came to London.

Harriot Mellon who married Mr Coutts

By this time Thomas Coutts had for many years been senior partner of Coutts & Co, bankers at 59 The Strand. Although his story is by no means one of rags to riches, his branch of the Coutts family had come a long way, geographically and economically, from their roots. The surname, variously spelt, first appears in the north of Scotland in the papers of the Keeper of the Archives (Chartulary) of Moray, in 1343, noticing Richard de Cotis as a landowner. A hundred years later a Coutts family are '*named in the Earldom of Mar in Aberdeenshire of the lands of Ochtercoul.*' In the seventeenth century the Coutts were merchants in Auchtercoul in Montrose, Scotland. Many had become Provost of their community.

John Coutts, born July 1699, moved to Edinburgh in 1723. There he set up as banker and corn merchant and was so successful that he became Baillie of Edinburgh in 1731 to 1741 (the equivalent in England being an Alderman) and Lord Provost of Edinburgh from 1742 to 1744. A hundred years later a copy of his portrait by Allan Ramsay was presented to the Corporation of Edinburgh by Baroness Burdett-Coutts. After the untimely death in 1749 of John Coutts, his four sons renamed the firm as Coutts Brothers. They established a branch in the City of London, managed by Patrick and Thomas, while John and James remained in Edinburgh. In 1692 a Scot, John Campbell had founded a bank in the Strand in which his son George became senior partner in 1727. James Coutts, on a visit to his brothers in London, met George Campbell on whom he made a very good impression. The Coutts and Campbell families were linked, since Patrick Coutts married Jean, widow of Robert Campbell of Hillhead, who became the mother of John and grandmother of the Coutts brothers.

In 1755 James married Mary (Polly) Peagrim, granddaughter of the founder, and became a partner in the bank. Within five years Polly and her uncle George Campbell had died and the widowed James took his brother Thomas into the partnership and brought down their capital from Edinburgh to put into the new bank. In spite of this great opportunity sadness followed during the next year, when John died in Edinburgh and Patrick became insane. Other troubles followed for James, who disapproved of his nursemaid Susannah Starkie marrying Thomas in 1763, and began to resent his brother's greater ability. Thomas did indeed prove to be an exceptionally able banker for he brought £4,000 into the bank when he entered partnership and when he died left a fortune of £100,000. James began to dabble in politics and he too became mentally ill, so that by 1775 he was persuaded to retire from the partnership.

Although Thomas took partners only his name remained in the title of the bank. Thomas' marriage to Susannah Starkie brought them three daughters, so beautiful that they were known, and painted, as 'The Three Graces.'

"The Three Graces"

All three married well. The eldest, Susan, married, in 1796, George Augustus, 3rd Earl of Guildford, son of Lord North, the Prime Minister. She died 1837 and was survived by her daughter Susan, Baroness North. Frances, the second daughter, married in 1800 John first Marquis of Bute, son of John, Earl of Bute, KG, first Lord of the Treasury. Frances was his second wife. She died in 1832 leaving a son, Lord Dudley Coutts Stuart who married a daughter of Lucienne Bonaparte the Prince of Canino. She also left a daughter Frances, who married Dudley Ryder, 2nd Earl of Harrowby.

Sophia, the youngest, married in 1793 Sir Francis Burdett, 5th Baronet, of Foremark in the county of Derby. Thomas Coutts gave him the rotten borough of Boroughbridge in Yorkshire, which he had bought from the Duke of Newcastle for £4,000 in 1797. Francis Burdett refused to join either the Whigs or the Tories, acting as an Independent. Sophia died in 1844 leaving one son and five daughters. The youngest, Angela Georgina, always a favourite of Harriot's, inherited her large fortune. Angela Burdett assumed the additional surname and arms of Coutts and was created Baroness Burdett-Coutts in 1871.

Thomas' first wife Susannah died in 1815 and four days after her funeral Thomas, by then aged 70, married Harriot, secretly at St Pancras on 18 January 1815. The marriage was concealed from Thomas' daughters until the end of February, and was then announced in *The Times* on Friday 3 March. To appease family disapproval Thomas and Harriot went through another marriage ceremony on 12 April but always kept the first date as their anniversary. The marriage contract stated that all Harriot's estates and money should remain always and entirely at her own disposal and command, the same as if she were still unmarried, just as Thomas had advised her, several years previously. Thomas also settled on her an annuity of £1,000 clear of tax. Nevertheless, Harriot spent her own money on buying town houses for her husband's family to use at 1 Stratton Street and 78 Piccadilly. At the same time Thomas gave money to the estate for his daughters so that family hostility to the marriage was somewhat lessened.

One of Harriot's most engaging characteristics was her fondness for children. She always kept four pretty little beds for the granddaughters and enjoyed games with them in her 'rumpus room' at her house in Highgate. It was here, in Holly Lodge, that Thomas and Harriot spent most of their time after their marriage. They entertained lavishly here, their guests including the Prince of Wales and the Dukes of York, Kent and Clarence. This friendly connection with the royal family must have annoyed Thomas' daughter Susan, who had offered to present Harriot at Court on her marriage, believing that Queen Charlotte would refuse to receive her. In the event Harriot was received with *'most marked kindness'* by the Prince Regent. Harriot's mother lived to see her daughter so advantageously married, dying in May 1815. Harriot, forgetting the hard times remembered her mother in a handsome memorial in her church in Cheltenham.

Harriot, who showed great generosity throughout her life, must have been distressed to find herself often accused of a lavish life style and giving charity for show. This however, can be seen to be less than just from several instances of her secret gifts on many occasions when she was first earning. From early days at Drury Lane she sent money to Mr Wright, her friend, the banker in Stafford to distribute to prisoners there and made a life-long allowance to her theatre dresser. On winning a lottery around 1808 she gave away part to the Drury Lane and Covent Garden Fund, and was rewarded by a flood of begging letters. In 1814 she became an anonymous benefactor to Edmund Kean and on a later occasion she kept silent about her offer of a large sum of money to Sir Walter Scott, then old and poor. Though not accepting her offer, he described her as a *'kind friendly woman, without affectation or insolence in the display of her wealth.'* Scott remained a good friend whose advice she sought, after the death of Thomas, about marrying the Duke of St Albans, whom she had taken to visit him. Although many criticised the marriage Scott offered no objections to it. She asked him to write her life and presented him with a pen and inkstand, which still remains in house at Abbotsford, although he never wrote her story.

There was certainly an element of theatricality about her invitations to beggars to a charity table at the gates of Holly Lodge, until her husband objected. More privately, she sent gifts and money to Ireland to relieve distress and blankets and coal in winter to the poorest districts of London. Towards the end of her life, when in 1836 there was severe distress among the Spittalfields weavers, Harriot subscribed publicly the same amount as the Queen. Privately, however, she also supported the weavers by ordering five hundred yards of their material at one guinea a yard in order to have new curtains made for the sitting rooms in Stratton Street. Emphasizing her support, she had her dresses made from these weavers' materials.

Within the family, she was extremely generous to her step-daughters in spite of their hostility. This was sometimes so virulent that Thomas often asked her not to plead for them as they had acted with so much unkindness after the marriage. Forgiving the ill treatment which she had received as a child Harriot supported her ageing mother with great generosity. Harriot's affection for Thomas showed itself during his last illness through her great concern about his treatment. She frequently questioned the doctors and nurses who were continually taking offence. Thomas died on 24 February 1822 leaving Harriot his whole fortune of £900,000 (£68 million in 2007) and his half share in the bank. She gave each of Thomas' daughters £10,000 a year and left them each £20,000 in her will.

Harriot Coutts entered the partnership of Coutts & Co in the year when Thomas died. Among clients of the bank were some whose connection would appear to be through Harriot, including theatrical names such as Richard Sheridan, Macready, Henry Irving, William Gilbert and Richard D'Oyley Carte. Mrs Jordan was introduced by the Duke of Clarence. Other famous names found on the books of the bank were Frederic Chopin, Lord Leighton and several authors, Walter Scott, Wilkie Collins, Harrison Ainsworth, Alfred Lord Tennyson and in 1847 the first of the Sitwells.

For the rest of Harriot's long life she continued as an independent banker. Despite her second marriage in 1827 to the 9th Duke of St Albans, she never admitted him to the bank partnership. At the time she joined the bank, the other partners were Sir Coutts Trotter, whom some sources say remained senior partner, Sir Edmund Antrobus and Edward Marjoribanks. Harriot is known to have scrutinized the books regularly and exercised her right to appoint new partners. She refused a Trotter nephew (which would indicate her seniority in the bank) but appointed Andrew Dickie, who had been confidential clerk to her late husband. If her partners, like those in Child's bank, believed in the promotion of long-serving clerks, this appointment should have been very acceptable to them, as, one might have supposed, it would have been to the clerks themselves. It was said, however, that she was not a favourite with the clerks, '*being, they considered, something of a bore.*' Indeed, too keen an interest by the management cannot be always welcomed.

By 1830 the money that each Coutts partner could draw annually shows the hierarchy at the bank. Edward Marjoribanks drew £20,000, Sir Coutts Trotter and Sir Edmund Antrobus £25,000 each and Harriot £80,000. In 2007 this latter amount would represent £5.8 million. The figure adds evidence to the general view at the time that two of the richest bankers in London were peeresses, the Duchess of St Albans and the Countess of Jersey. They both enjoyed a reputation for going regularly to their respective banks, where they took a keen interest, general and detailed. They were active in promoting and dismissing partners which is not altogether consistent with the description of them as '*distinguished by the affability and good sense with which they sustained their position.*'

A London bank of the period. Coutts office sketch

Harriot had spent the first five years of widowhood immersed in her work at the bank. In 1827, shock and amazement greeted the announcement of her marriage, at the age of fifty, to a man twenty-four years her junior, William Aubrey de Vere, 9th Duke of St Albans. This unlikely couple met when the then Lord Burford was only twenty-three, their mutual attraction based on a common love of Shakespeare. His father encouraged the connection, though in fact they did not marry until after his death. They both enjoyed entertaining and were accused of giving lavish parties at Stratton Street and Holly Lodge, no doubt by those who were not invited. Nor did this extravagance affect her plan to leave Thomas Coutts' capital to his descendants, for she was able easily to pay for the parties out of her earnings. Her generous plan, however, ran into difficulties, for she disapproved of most of Thomas' grandchildren for various reasons. For instance, she considered Lord Dudley Coutts-Stuart unpatriotic for marrying a niece of Napoleon. At her death in 1837 she therefore left all the money to Angela Burdett, the youngest child of Thomas' youngest daughter, Sophia, on condition that she took additionally the name of Coutts and did not marry an alien.

Angela was neglected by her mother and used often to visit Harriot, who took pleasure in her company and in buying her pretty dresses. Harriot so greatly admired her niece's forceful character that she also left Angela the Coutts bank. Unlike her aunt, Angela, however, did not become an active partner but was a noted philanthropist and was created Baroness in 1871.

In 1881, aged fifty-seven, Angela married an American, Ashmead Bartlett. Because of the terms of Harriot's will, Clara Money, Angela's elder sister, took her to court, on the grounds that an American was an alien. The trustees eventually divided the money between the two sisters, and on their deaths it went to Clara's son, Francis Money Coutts, who became 5th Baron Latimer. He was not a partner in the bank, though his children and grandchildren continued in the family tradition.

Harriot would have been pleased to find that Thomas' descendants still continued to carry on their family bank and that his name is still prominent in banking. Coutts, having become a company, returned to partnership with unlimited liability following a crisis in Baring's Bank. By the 1920s it had become a subsidiary of the National Provincial Bank, later the National Westminster, later NatWest Bank. In 2000 it was bought by the Royal Bank of Scotland in the largest corporate transaction ever known in the European banking sector. In 2006 Coutts was part of the Wealth Management division of the Royal Bank of Scotland, and at that time a Coutts automatic teller machine was installed in the basement of Buckingham Palace for the use of the royal family.

Harriot Coutts' long life with its many contradictory stages gave scope to a many-sided personality. She was absurdly superstitious and to avoid ill luck always kept a copy of Queen Catherine Parr's *Prayers or Meditations* (1545) with her. She would never sit down thirteen at table, nor make plans for Twelfth Night, yet in spite of such vagaries, she never lost her excellent head for business. Nonetheless, essentially prudent, she could thoroughly enjoyed extravagance but in spite of great social success Harriot never ceased to understand the value of respectability.

These three histories show that success could come from very different social upbringing, which ranged from a prosperous London trader, through an aristocratic nursery, to a child actress with a single parent. They were alike in appreciating the luxury that business success brought, and each was able to keep her independent career, without including her second husband in her bank partnership.

Chapter Two

Founders and Opening Partnerships

There are eight women who were in the opening partnership of a bank. Two of these founded their banks, **ANN BUTLIN** and **MARGARET CAMPION**.

Founders: **ANN BUTLIN**, Rugby (later joined by daughters Catherine Butlin and Maria Benn).

In the early 1790s, in Rugby, Ann Butlin, whose husband William, a draper, had recently died, developed a profitable banking business. The bank first appeared in 1791 as A. Butlin & Son, and continued to be listed as such in the directories. An article in the *Rugby Advertiser* of 7 July 1961 describes Ann, the widow of William Butlin, as '*Rugby's first banker.*' When the bank applied for a licence to issue promissory notes in 1812 the partners' names are Ann Butlin and William Butlin (Ann's son). By 1846 Ann's son James and daughters Catherine and Maria had joined. Maria married Thomas Benn, who on his death in 1821 left his half share in '*the family's bank of A. Butlin & Son*' to her. She had four small sons and was pregnant, with George, her fifth. Maria and her family lived at Benfield in North Street, later occupied by a branch of Barclays Bank. In 1848 James Butlin of Westfield House was in partnership with his sisters '*Maria Benn & Catherine Butlin*' and the bank continued to be carried on as a family business.

All five of Maria Benn's sons went to Rugby School, and two of them entered the bank. None of them married, and each in turn left his money to their youngest brother George. Maria Benn continued the matriarchal tradition, but without bringing new blood into the bank the situation could not last and when Lloyds bought the bank in 1868 for £15,000, *'the partners were elderly, rich and no younger generation coming along.'* George Benn *'retired as a gentleman of leisure.'* Maria, however, lived to enjoy the fruits of the sale of her bank for more than ten years' before her death in 1881. Her son George used the bank profits to make generous benefactions to Rugby, including the bell tower and spire of the church as well as the Benn Memorial Hall. *'He left the Shoulder of Mutton Inn in High Street and £6,000 to build council offices, which were used until 1937, but are now (2000) the site of Marks and Spencers.'* The last survivor of the partners in Ann Butlin & Son, he died in 1895, more than 100 years after his grandmother had founded the bank, which had succeeded so well that his estate at death was valued at £624,000 which equates to £51.5 million pounds in 2007.

MARGARET CAMPION, WHITBY.

Margaret Campion was the daughter of John Holt, coming from a long line of ship-owners in Whitby, who were also involved in subsidiary trades such as flax dressing, sailcloth weaving and bleaching in their mills at Bagdale. The Holt family was connected by marriage with the Chapmans, a local landed family when Esther, daughter of Abe Chapman, founder of the Whitby bank, married Thomas Holt. Their eldest daughter Martha married her cousin Edward Chapman in 1794 and their son Thomas inherited the Chapman estate. A generation later, in 1840, Margaret's great-granddaughter Ann reinforced the family connection when she married back into the Chapmans. The Holts were thus linked with shipping, with banking and with local landowners. Margaret's brothers owned ships, as did her husband, Nathaniel Campion. Her sisters married local bankers; Mary with Charles Richardson, a banker in Whitby, becoming a partner in his bank, and Elizabeth with Joseph Atty, the owner of a whale-processing factory in Whitby and a banker in Stockton on Tees. After her husband's death in 1798 making it easier to trade in her own right, Margaret brought together the several businesses in which her family engaged. She continued trading overseas, paying the fee to become a Freeman in the Russia Company. This entitled her to engage in the lucrative Baltic trade, twenty per cent of which was carried by Whitby, and in which many Whitby families involved themselves. This had also its considerable dangers. In 1800 the crazed Russian Emperor Paul seized British ships and goods, forcing the ships companies to march weary miles into the interior of Russia, often in great distress, where very many died of exposure and privation. Whether by skill or good fortune, none of Margaret's immediate connections, neither the Holts nor the Campions nor the Chapmans, were involved in the losses caused to many Whitby traders by this despotic act.

Bank founder Margaret Campion, Freeman in the Russia Company

At this time Margaret bravely embarked upon a new venture, opening a bank, along with her twenty-six year-old son Robert on 2 January 1800, a time when Whitby was the seventh largest port in Britain offering plenty of scope to a banker. She continued successfully to operate her bank and her ships and was able to celebrate the birth of her grandson John in 1803, but died on 15 February the following year, when Robert became sole partner in the bank. In the course of the next twenty years, after adding a wine business, Robert gained the reputation of being one of the richest men in Whitby and by 1826 claimed the title of *'Esq, of Bagdale,'* the place where they had their sailcloth factory. The claim to squiredom, not automatically made at the time, was perhaps suggested to him by the family relationship to the land-owning Chapmans.

It was unfortunate that Robert should have apparently become more interested in his position as a gentleman than in working for his bank. Nor did his son John, who joined him in the bank, seem prepared to take any greater responsibility for the business, with the result that it failed, as R and J Campion, for no small amount, in the crisis of 1841. Later, Joseph Sykes, a bank historian, was to write that a Whitby bank had been founded by *'a lady of the name of Margaret Campion'* implying that she was the obvious cause of the failure. He preferred to ignore the fact that she had been dead for nearly forty years and could not, without perversity, be held responsible for the 1841 disaster. Perhaps however, she should incur some blame for failing to bring up her son in a stronger work ethic. Apparently undaunted by the failure, Robert lived on to the great age of ninety-three. John, described as *'gentleman'* in directories in spite of the crash, entered a new profession, was ordained by the Archbishop of Canterbury at Lambeth in 1845, dying in 1894 aged ninety-one.

Margaret Campion and her bank illustrate many of the characteristics common to country bankers as a whole. As in many places, the partners were prominent in the strongest trades of the town, which in Whitby was the ownership of trading vessels and the manufacture of sailcloth. Also typically, the partners in this bank were related by birth or marriage to others in the same or different banks, in the same or other towns, as were three quarters of all provincial private bankers. The strength afforded by such close family links could be offset through the very nature of families, where not all members are equally business-like. Margaret Campion offers an unhappy example of the dangers inherent in such a family bank, in which, after her death, too great a reliance was placed on weak family members working without any more disciplined influence from other clearer sighted and unrelated partners.

OPENING PARTNERSHIPS: HANNAH HASLEHURST, SHEFFIELD; OLIVE BEDWELL, CIRENCESTER; SARAH, REBECCA AND HANNAH DARBY, COALBROOKDALE; REBECCA DREWRY, PENRITH.

When a woman is named in the earliest entry for a bank, it has been assumed that she is a founder. In one instance the woman banker appears only in a list of bankruptcies, in another she failed after six years in banking. Of the other six founders, one ceased without loss after a short time and the other five carried on successfully for many years.

HANNAH HASLEHURST. The earliest provincial banker, Hannah Haslehurst, is known from the London Gazette entry of 31 August 1784: *'Hannah Haslehurst and George Haslehurst, bankrupt as bankers at Sheffield.'* As Hannah is listed first, it is likely that she was in partnership with her son, and may well have added banking to some other enterprise. The Haslehurst family was active in many fields in the town and other members were evidently not disastrously affected by the bank failure. In the first half of the nineteenth century they appear in directories as taverners, iron-merchants, brewers, engravers and gardeners, and in 1834 Mrs Mary Haslehurst is listed as a *'gentlewoman.'*

OLIVE BEDWELL. Bedwell and Williamson appear as bankers and mercers in the *Universal British Directory* for 1790. The early banks in Cirencester seem to have been set up through *'the custom of the ancient Weavers' Guild to accommodate members with loans for business at a rate of interest of 5%.'* The name Bedwell occurs in many entries in Cirencester eighteenth century records. These show a John and Frances Bedwell at Hathrup in 1776. A John Bedwell, mercer, died in 1790 and another John Bedwell and his sons were bankers in Cheltenham between 1790 and their bankruptcy was recorded in 1798. In the London Gazette of 1792 Olive Bedwell *'declines banking business lately carried on by her at the Old Bank in Cirencester.'* Her partner in the bank, John Williamson, continued, with new partners, until 1794.

SARAH DARBY, REBECCA DARBY, HANNAH DARBY. Three women, Sarah, Rebecca and Hannah Darby, were founding partners in the Coalbrookdale bank near Ironbridge, Shropshire. They were friends of Elizabeth Fry, the Quaker reformer and preacher, and were themselves active in the Society of Friends. All were related by birth or marriage to the Quaker iron-master, Abraham Darby, and two had been partners for many years in the iron works, the Dale company, before the formation of the bank. Elizabeth Gurney (later Elizabeth Fry) described them as *'all ready at any time to take an interest in the business management and actual working of the Dale company.'*

Abraham Darby III, the builder of the celebrated iron bridge, linked these three women, and must also have known the Quaker bankers at Falmouth, where he had built a warehouse to accommodate the increasing Cornish trade. A strong vein of independence ran through the family; Abraham's father was left an orphan when six years old, and perhaps encouraged by his own career to consider that youth was no bar to success, when he died in 1763 he left the works to his thirteen-year-old son. His son-in-law, the iron-master Richard Reynolds, moved from his own works at Ketley to Dale House and took the young Abraham as his apprentice. When he was eighteen, Abraham took over the management of the works, with the help of the older workmen to whom he became an excellent master. One of the workmen, who had known Abraham's grandfather, said of him that he *'liked a joke right well, and as for kindness, it seemed as if he thought it a favour to be allowed to assist you.'* Abraham III rapidly modernized the works, installing new machinery, though still holding to old-fashioned business morality. In 1775, ignoring the effects of the war on the price of pig-iron, he and Reynolds refused the opportunity for profiteering and continued to make a fair price for their customers, by which they also made a fair profit for themselves. The company continued to prosper and by 1810 members of the family formed the Coalbrookdale Bank. This bank appears in Leekey's list of banks applying for a licence to issue notes in 1813, although some historians ignore this aspect of the Darby activities.

SARAH, Abraham Darby's younger sister, was for many years the mainstay of the family, as well as a partner in the company and in the bank. Soon after Abraham was born their parents, Abraham II and Abiah Maud from a Sunderland Quaker family, moved into the new house which they had built on the hill above Coalbrookdale which they named Sunnyside after Abiah's old home. It was a large house in local brick with stone facings, three floors with sash windows, and dormers in the roof. The buildings on the estate included malt-houses, brew-houses, barns, stables and several cottages. The large gardens ended in steeply sloping ground used as a small deer park, altogether a very substantial place. Sarah was born here on 24 August 1752, an event noted in her mother's diary: '*I was delivered of my Sally ... the Lord was good to me in this Tryal (sic) as heretofore.*' When Sarah was eight she had a near disastrous accident while riding pillion with a groom when the horse fell on her. Her mother gave thanks for her survival as of '*one raised from the dead.*' Sarah, however, received no coddling as a result, and when she was eight was sent off to boarding school, at John Fells in Worcester, with her brothers. Apart from her school terms, though, Sarah continued to live at Sunnyside, a constant and invaluable presence at the arrival of family babies, appearing as witness to the birth certificates of many nieces and nephews. It was she who looked after their widowed mother, and went often to London to take care of her brother Samuel during his mental breakdowns. On these occasions his wife Deborah, found that her own presence seemed only to make him worse.

It was in 1789, a disastrous year for the family, that Sarah showed herself a survivor. She and her brother Abraham caught scarlet fever, and in March, when he died, she was too ill to be told. Even at the end of April she could leave her bed only for a wheelchair, but nevertheless insisted on becoming a partner in Joseph Rathbone & the Dale Company. This operated as a trust, the partners putting back profits on the basis of a five per cent loan, and Sarah also contributed to the support of her brother Samuel's wife and children because of his continuing mental illness. Samuel remained a partner in the company until his death in 1797, though in 1793 Sarah, together with her sister, Mary Rathbone, arranged that money owed to them by the company should be used to 'exonerate' debts to the company by Samuel and their late brother Abraham. This was particularly generous as all the children of Abraham Darby II had inherited the same share in the company, Abraham III, Samuel, Sarah and Mary all receiving one fifth, the last share going to his son-in-law Richard Reynolds. The company owned a large amount of land, including two farms, one of which was worked by direct labour and the other rented by Sarah. Here she kept a team of horses which she hired out, and in another enterprise provided the malt to brew the beer for the workmen, although she herself did not take on the management of the brewery, a family business started by Abraham Darby. In 1797 when the partnership was dissolved after Samuel's death, Sarah remained a partner in the company though by 1802 though she had given up this partnership to her sister-in-law, Samuel's widow Deborah.

In 1810 Sarah was the senior partner in the newly-formed Coalbrookdale Bank. The next partner was her sister-in-law Rebecca, with her son Francis and his wife Hannah, her younger son Richard, and her son-in-law Barnard Dickenson. Mary Rathbone and Deborah Darby did not join the bank partnership, Deborah perhaps because she was too busy, for she became well-known as a preacher, having inspired her friend Elizabeth Gurney to follow the same vocation. Elizabeth stayed at Coalbrookdale in the summer of 1798, when John Gurney was taking his seven daughters on a long journey and stopped to rest there. Elizabeth Gurney, later the famous Elizabeth Fry, not being well, was left with the Darbys, finding them and their home very well suited to her state of mind, as she put it. Patronisingly, she went on to describe them as *'a group of widows who were struggling to keep on the company until their sons were old enough to take up the burden.'* The 'Darby wives' she summed up, were *'a remarkable group of women.'* This, though a handsome tribute to her hostesses, seems to take it for granted that the women were merely working as a stop-gap until their men folk could take over from them. Nor in using the term 'wives' did Elizabeth do justice to Sarah, that extremely hard-working but unmarried member of the family. By the time Sarah died, in 1821, many of her duties had, however, long been shared with her sister-in-law, Rebecca.

REBECCA DARBY was born in 1752, the same year as Sarah. She was the daughter of Francis Smith of Doncaster, a well-to-do grocer, and Ruth Gulson, of the Coventry Quaker family, members of which were partners in the Coventry bank of Eagle & Co. Her aunt, also Rebecca, was Richard Reynolds' second wife, with whom she had often stayed at Dale House. Here she and Abraham met as children, and married in 1776, a union approved by their relations, for the families had known each other for more than a generation. Abraham's family considered that Rebecca had been so well educated, and was so 'sensible' that she would be a great help to her husband in his business.

Dale House, overlooking the original furnaces, became their first home. In 1780 they moved to The Haye, a much larger house, with its own home farm, at the other end of the Severn Gorge. This house was perhaps not so plain as might be expected in a Quaker home, for they had silk upholstery in the parlour, and used a handsome Nanking dinner service, accompanied by elegant table silver, when they entertained the many visitors who came to see the bridge. Rebecca was not able to enjoy this style of life for long, as the reckoning came when Abraham Darby died in 1789, only thirty-nine years old and intestate, and she had to sell the house and its fine contents, and move with the children into the small White House in Coalbrookdale. Not content with merely economising, Rebecca entered the ironworks partnership in her husband's place, continuing active in it for many years, her partners being Sarah and three other members of the Darby family. In 1790, the year after Abraham Darby's death, a question was raised as to the advantages of merging the Dale Company with Richard Reynolds' son's partnership, William Reynolds & Co. There was a doubt whether Rebecca, as executor, had the right to vote, a question which their solicitor solved in 1791 by giving it as his opinion that as administrator of her late husband's estate she was entitled to cast her vote. The Dale Company had to pay debts incurred by the unfortunate Samuel, and by Rebecca's own husband's too impulsive extravagances. Nobody would have quibbled at the cost of the Meeting House he had built at New Dale, but Rebecca must have been embarrassed that Sarah and Mary, had to 'exonerate'—pay for—the elegancies of The Haye drawing room, although their inherited share in the company was no larger than her own.

After the re-formation of the company partnership in 1797, and even more after Sarah retired in 1802, Rebecca repaid her sisters-in-law for their generosity by continuing to carry the responsibility of the senior partner in the Dale company. Rebecca's death in 1834 came two years before their partnership, with other bankers in the county, formed the Shropshire Banking Company, which was absorbed by Lloyd's Bank in 1874. Rebecca amply justified Elizabeth Fry's commendation of the 'Darby wives.' So in a more limited way did Rebecca's daughter-in-law, Hannah. She illustrates the frequent connection between country bankers.

HANNAH DARBY, (*see also Chapter 3*) the daughter of Hannah Grant, a Quaker banker at Leighton Buzzard, married Rebecca's son Francis and with him became a founding partner in the Coalbrookdale Bank, though not in the Dale company. With her mother's example, she would certainly see nothing remarkable in a woman becoming a banker. Hannah remained in the town after the bank had formed a joint stock company, living with her mother and her daughter Adelaide. She occupied the White House until her death in 1860, the last survivor of that remarkable group of women.

REBECCA DREWRY. The energetic Rebecca Drewry, sadly, missed the time when she might have flourished as a banker. She was 'proprietor' not only of a bank but also of a grocery and a coal mine. She opened and carried on a bank in Penrith nearly thirty years later than the Darbys had in Coalbrookdale. Rebecca's husband, Joseph, died in 1830, leaving her with four children. He was a successful grocer, not a banker though there is some evidence that he may have occasionally lent money on securities. Rebecca saw an opportunity to develop this line of business, and is first listed as a banker in a directory of 1834. Rebecca was at that date proprietor of the grocer's shop which was '*in the most central part of town and had always commanded the best custom.*' A customer's invoice shows that she sold '*wholesale and retail teas, genuine as imported, spices, foreign fruit and hops etc., wax, mould and dip candles, roasted coffee, plain and cut glass in great variety, and British wines.*' A sort of local Harrods, perhaps.

Overseeing her varied business interests must have involved her in much travelling, for her coal mine was at Weary Hall, in the parish of Bolton, nearly twenty miles from Penrith, at a date when forty-miles round trip over country roads can have been no easy day's work. It was to this multiplicity of interests that Rebecca's failure in 1840 was attributed. Her enterprise was described as '*the business of a grocer, damaged by that of a coal mine and the practice of banking and ruined by speculation in both of these employments.*' She succeeded, however, in paying sixteen shillings in the pound in three years on £18,000 being the debts of her business. Two at least of her children contributed to the repayment of creditors. Thomas and William made over property for this purpose in May 1841. After her bankruptcy no other private bank replaced her and only joint stock or savings banks now remained in the town. Mastermans, who had been her London agent, continued their connection with Penrith by acting for a banker from a nearby town who found it sufficient '*to attend on Tuesdays at the George Inn.*' Mrs Drewry had, in fact, chosen a dangerous time to embark on a private partnership bank, for the general failure of confidence in the 1840s proved disastrous for very many businesses which might otherwise have prospered.

Chapter Three

Wives in partnership with their husbands

ELIZABETH EVANS, DERBY; HANNAH DARBY, COALBROOKDALE; MARY MASSEY, KINGS LYNN; JANE MORRIS, STAINES; ELIZABETH MUSGRAVE, WINCANTON; ANN FAWTHORPE SMITH, STOCKTON; ELIZABETH LUTENER, SHREWSBURY.

ELIZABETH EVANS. Elizabeth Evans of Derby enjoyed the unique position of entering the bank with her second husband Walter after the death of her first husband, William, Walter's half-brother. The partnership formed an extended family group with her father-in-law, Thomas and her son William Evans junior and her brother William Strutt. In this dynamic situation she showed her forceful personality and reforming zeal.

This could be seen as the result of a childhood moulded by her character-forming father, Jedediah Strutt. The son of a small farmer at Alfreton, but a keen student, he invented the Derby Rib Machine for making stockings. He later became a partner of Richard Arkwright, the pioneer in cotton manufacturing. Jedediah was kept busy organizing not only the great mills he had opened in Derbyshire, but also the sales side of his business in London. His wife died while she was with him there in May 1774. Jedediah did not return to Derby for nine months after her death. Although his energy and zeal in business are admirable, the reverse is true of his behaviour as a father. He left his daughter Elizabeth, still only sixteen years old, in charge of house, dairy and farm, as well as a string of younger siblings, William, Martha, George and Joe.

Seeing William's potential, Elizabeth kept him busy at his lessons. Justifying her confidence William was in due course elected a Fellow of the Royal Society. She took her responsibilities very seriously. A letter to her father complained that Alice, the maid, did not do the washing well and their clothes were not so good a colour as they used to be. On the other hand, she could boast that the butter they were making had a much better taste than previously, and, there was a new arrival: a '*pretty pig.*'

In answer to her letter telling him that she enjoyed the books he had sent '*vastly*' her father wrote reprovingly that the word was most inelegant. The poor girl was not only questioned about her book-learning and French lessons, but criticised on more personal grounds, for lisping, being bashful in company, and staying too long in bed. Elizabeth accepted the criticism and in addition to all these faults, blamed herself for envying her pretty little sister Martha for her air of ease and her graceful dancing. She wrote to assure her father that she now got up at 5 o'clock in the morning and that she would be '*diligent, temperate and virtuous.*' '*I will love the truth*' she wrote, '*I cannot say that I will be wise, but I shall endeavour to improve, to learn and know all that I can.*' It is pleasant to learn that Elizabeth had some relief from this arduous programme when her uncle William Strutt took her riding, in spite of his preoccupation with his own textile business.

In 1781 Jedediah married again, a widow whom the children felt to be '*below them.*' He and his new wife lived in Milford House, near one of his mills, while the children of his first marriage remained in Elizabeth's care in the house in Derby. Four years later, at the age of twenty-seven, Elizabeth gave up one set of responsibilities for another, when in 1785 she married William Evans, three years older than herself, the elder son of Thomas Evans, who had founded a Derby bank in 1771. Thomas did not, however, confine himself to banking, being also in local navigation, a tinplate manufacturer, a raff (or timber) merchant and the proprietor of paper mills at Darley. His sons, half brothers William and Walter, were partners in the bank with him by 1780. On her marriage to William, Elizabeth was immediately faced with the duties of caring for a child, her husband's illegitimate son, Samuel, born the year of their marriage, whom she brought up with her own children, though '*not as an eldest son*' as the entry in *Burke's Landed Gentry* makes clear, listing Samuel as the second son.

Elizabeth soon had her own children; the education of her eldest, Bessie, born the year after her marriage, was entrusted to the Misses Mary and Susan Parker, the illegitimate daughters of Erasmus Darwin. Elizabeth's eldest son, William, born two years after Bessie was followed by Francis, Ellen, and two sons who died young. While on a visit to Yorkshire, George, aged only fifteen, dived too deep into a weir on the river Wharf and Thomas, born in 1796, the year of his father's death, lived only two years.

Widowed, and left with six children to care for, and further distressed by the death of little Thomas as well as that of her father, Elizabeth became ill. Her uncle William took her to Bath to recover, and on her return she resumed her normal active life, and began to look for a tutor for the children. Samuel Taylor Coleridge, a friend of another Derby banking family, the Cromptons, applied successfully to be considered, and he and his wife spent five weeks in Elizabeth's family. Mrs Coleridge was expecting a child and Elizabeth with her usual kind concerns gave her some of the baby clothes she had kept by her. Coleridge wrote to a friend that Mrs Evans is *without exception, the greatest woman I have been fortunate enough to meet with.* However, the children's guardians, including her late husband's half-brother Walter—perhaps fearing a scandal—persuaded her not to engage Coleridge as tutor. Walter, in his wish to protect her more effectively, then proposed marriage and was accepted. Coleridge was greatly concerned when he heard of it. He wrote to a friend *Oh God! Oh God! I wish—but what is the use of wishing? I wish that Walter Evans may have talent enough to appreciate Mrs Evans, but I suspect that his intellect is not tall enough to measure hers.*

Elizabeth, whether or not Walter's intellect may have measured hers, took on a new lease of life. She and Walter had a son, Arthur, and with Walter she began to take an active interest in the family bank in which she had been appointed a partner on the death of her first husband. The house at Darley Abbey, where many of the Evans' business interests lay became Elizabeth and Walter's home. The cotton manufactory was built there in 1783 *through Mr Arkwright's recommendation to the late Mr Thomas Evans and his son,* and that he accepted a compliment of £100 when the mill *proved a success.* Both the Evans and the Strutt families cared for the moral and spiritual welfare of the workers in their cotton factories as well as for the profits to be made from them.

Elizabeth wrote on the subject of *"the diffusion of knowledge and morals among the poor"* that *'the manufacturer has it considerably in his power to promote'* and *'is culpable in the neglect of it.'* None of Elizabeth's family failed in their self-imposed duty in this respect, implementing it by building a church and a school on the site. Nor did they neglect the physical comfort of their work-people, for whom they built cottages, and saw that these were well maintained. Lime was provided for white-washing, and teams of painters were always at work. In the winter, plaid shawls were given to the mill girls, though blankets were loaned. Each autumn a blanket was provided on payment of a shilling deposit, which was given back when the blankets were returned for washing next spring. Clearly, Elizabeth could enhance kindness with prudence. This tradition was carried on by Samuel, the baby Elizabeth brought up, her first husband's little love-child. The skill she had perforce acquired in bringing up her brother William, no doubt also helped Samuel. He carried on the cotton factory and paper mills at Darley, continuing his foster-mother's tradition of practical improvement in the workers' village, installing a sewage disposal system, enabling Darley to become the first village to benefit from such a novelty.

Samuel was also an active partner in the bank with Elizabeth, later taking on a directorship after its amalgamation with the Cromptons into a joint stock bank, adding to all this activity the position of High Sheriff of Derbyshire. Meanwhile, his half brother, Elizabeth's own son William, taking less interest in the bank, was created Knight of the Shire, and settled into country life as Sir William of Allestree Hall, giving Elizabeth good cause to be pleased with her son and step-son.

Elizabeth herself continued in the bank partnership for twelve years, retiring at the end of 1808. She gradually gave up partnership in the other Evans businesses and had completely retired by 1810, after which she enjoyed twenty-six years of happy retirement, dying at the age of seventy-eight, in 1836. That her long retirement was a happy one is proved by the memories she left in her family. After her death she was commemorated by her granddaughter with a phrase more complimentary even than her description, so many years ago, by Coleridge. Mrs Curtis wrote of her grandmother that she was *'a woman of extraordinary charm and power,'* an epitaph that any business woman might well envy.

HANNAH DARBY, *see Chapter 2.*

MARY MASSEY. Mary Massey appears with her husband Benjamin at King's Lynn in Leekey's list of 1813 as Massey & Co. This bank is first listed, as Gales & Co in 1808 and in the following year as Gales, Dixon & Massey, from which date it can be assumed that Mary and Benjamin had joined the partnership. Mary retired before 1830, when Twigg's list was published, though Benjamin continued until 1845 as a partner in this bank. The bank failed in 1888 at least fifty-five years since Mary Massey's name disappeared from the partnership.

JANE MORRIS. The Staines Bank of Coggan, Morris & Co. which was in business in 1810, was dissolved as John Coggan, John Morris and Sir William Abdy, Bart at the end of December that year. The notice of John Coggan's bankruptcy at Staines and Laleham had appeared in January 1812 but the revival of the bank as Jane and John Morris, with Jane Morris as senior partner enabled it to continue under the title of the Middlesex and Surrey Bank in both 1812 and 1813. Being junior partner at these dates, John Morris could have been her son. This bank is not shown at Staines in Pigot's directory of 1824.

ELIZABETH MUSGRAVE. The Wincanton bank of Musgrave, Garrett & Co. appears in a directory of 1809. Elizabeth Musgrave was in partnership there with her husband George in 1812. Elizabeth had ceased to be a partner before 1827 when the bank failed as Thomas Garrett and John Clitson Musgrave, probably her son. A John Musgrave was Postmaster at Wincanton many years later, from 1840 to 1852.

ANN FAWTHORPE SMITH. At Stockton-on-Tees Ann Fawthorpe Smith was in partnership with her husband William. They are named in 1817 by Edward Beaumont, a witness to the Select Committee on Extents in Aid. Extents in Aid could be used by Crown debtors to obtain their payment of debts ahead of other creditors. At this date Sir Charles Price & Co, London bankers, issued an Extent *'against the house of William and Ann Smith for the recovery of two bills, one for £12,500 and the other for £7,000, both of which were indeed paid when they fell due.'* The use of an Extent could on occasion be less than scrupulous as suggested by the following answers.

When Charles Price was asked whether he was aware that he was a Crown Debtor at the time that William Smith & Co became indebted to him he replied that he did, *'but not such as had the right of issuing an Extent.'* Smith & Co were therefore unaware when they took out loans that this sanction could be used against them. Questioning continuing *'Are you aware what proportion of the effects of William Smith & Co were taken under the Extent in Aid? — A very small proportion; we had done the process as lenient as possible. Are you aware what diminution of the dividends of that house was occasioned by taking its property under the Extent?—I do not apprehend any. We have just taken possession. The property remains as it was, almost. There has been a trifling sale of the furniture of one of the private partners.'* We can surmise that poor Mrs. Smith did not consider this trifling.

ELIZABETH LUTENER, executor/partner. Elizabeth Lutener is listed in 1830 by Twigg with her husband William at Shrewsbury, as the Salop and North Wales Bank. They were serving as trustees and executors of Edward Hughes, deceased, one of the founders of Price, Hughes & Co in 1825. This bank failed as Price & Co in 1841. It might be assumed that women taking part in the management of a bank alongside their husbands enjoyed a measure of reassurance from the partnership. On the other hand, the women found in this group seem not to have been strikingly more successful than their contemporaries who were banking without such support.

Chapter Four

Women in partnership with other relatives

CHRISTIANA MARIA AMPHLETT, DUDLEY; HANNAH SWAINE, HALIFAX; JANE ST AUBYN, DEVONPORT; ELIZABETH RUNDLE, TAVISTOCK; MARY SIMMONDS, ASHBY DE LA ZOUCHE; ELIZABETH BRADLEY, SANDWICH; KATHERINE HARVEY, SANDWICH; ANN HOWARD, RICKMANSWORTH; CATHERINE FOX, FALMOUTH; CATHERINE PAYTON FOX, FALMOUTH; ELIZABETH CARNE, PENZANCE.

CHRISTIANA MARIA AMPHLETT, Spinster with father; executor/partner. One aspect of the prejudice against which women had to contend is shockingly demonstrated by Christiana Amphlett's exit from her bank partnership. Christiana was the first spinster to take up banking, having been left the senior partnership, as his executor, in the Dudley bank of Dixon and Amphlett by her father Joseph in 1801. She was born on 30 September 1779, and baptised three months later at St Thomas' Church in Dudley, where she was later to be married. Her mother Mary Bree was the daughter of Robert Bree of Solihull. Her grandfather, William Amphlett, was a younger son who married his cousin, Christian Amphlett, daughter of John Amphlett of Clent. A possible connection between his family and the banker at Falmouth, Catherine Fox, may be found. Her uncle James Payton, lived in Dudley and died there in 1786, at a date when William Amphlett also lived in the town.

Joseph was born at the Amphlett manor house of Hadzor. Although a member of the local landowning family Joseph determined to be independent, so embarked upon a business career. He started a nail factory, as well as an ironmongery in Dudley High Street while still in his twenties and by 1790 had opened a bank in partnership with Edward Dixon. In addition to these activities, in company with Edward Dixon and William Bedford, a Birmingham solicitor, he bought an estate of over 300 acres at Horsley, Tipton, to develop the seam of coal under it. Joseph was appointed chief manager and director of the company, with a salary of £200 a year and authority to spend £600 to repair the house. He was also required to give up his nail manufactory but remained an ironmonger and a banker. He was a magistrate for Worcestershire and Staffordshire and Deputy Lieutenant for the latter county. He married his first wife Mary Bree, in 1778 and their only child was their daughter Christiana. Her mother died when she was only five years old and she was thirteen when her father married again and moved to Horsley House. Her new step-mother Mary was the daughter of her father's partner, Edward Dixon, and her half-brother born in 1794, was named Edward after his grandfather. Mary died only a month after the baby's birth, leaving the fifteen-year-old Christiana to care for her little brother, in somewhat similar circumstances to those of Elizabeth Evans at Derby.

Christiana so gained her father's confidence by the manner in which she fulfilled her duties that he felt able to leave her his partnership in the bank and make her his sole executor at his death six years later. On taking up her partnership, the first concern of this conscientious woman was to provide the bank clerks with '*decent mourning*.' Joseph Amphlett could not leave her the Horsley house, as he owned only one third of the property, which he instructed his partners, as trustees, to divide between his two children '*eventually*.' He did, however, bequeath Christiana all its contents, '*furniture, plate, china, linen, liquors, books, horses, carriages and live and dead stock of every description.*' He left to his son Edward, a house he owned in Snow Hill in the parish of Dudley which was let at the time. An odd provision in the will stated that if either of his children should not be satisfied with the division of the effects and should start legal proceedings the other should receive his whole third share in the Horsley estate. As his son was only six years old at his death, too young to become a litigant on his own account, it may be that he feared that his second wife's relations would not be satisfied with his son's share in the will.

Joseph probably knew already that his daughter would not long need a house as she was to marry the Revd Edward Dudley of Broome, Worcestershire, vicar of Kingswynford. The marriage was no doubt approved, as Edward Dudley was a connection of her mother's family and there had been many marriages between the Amphletts, the Brees and the Dudleys. The marriage, however, did not take place until 1803, after a period of mourning. Meanwhile Christiana was able to take an active part in the bank certainly for a year after her father's death, and possibly until February 1806. Regrettably, it soon became obvious that her husband was determined to dissociate his wife from the bank. Although not himself a partner in the bank, he signed as a witness to a notice appearing in 1806 in the London Gazette. It read *'the partnership which heretofore subsisted between Edward Dixon of Dudley, banker, and Joseph Amphlett, late of Horsley House in the parish of Tipton, banker, deceased, as bankers under the firm of Dixon & Amphlett, and which partnership was continued in the same firm by the said Edward Dixon and his sole executor Christiana Maria (now the wife of the Revd Edward Dudley of Broome, clerk,) from the death of the said Joseph Amphlett on 5th January 1801 until 31st December following, was dissolved on the last mentioned day. Witness the hands of the parties this 18 February 1806.'*

This long entry was signed as follows: *'Edward Dixon, Edward Dudley, C M Dudley executrix of my late father Joseph Amphlett, deceased.'* It is certainly not usual for such a notice to be signed by anyone other than a partner or executor. This unwarranted intervention by Edward Dudley was presumably aimed at putting an end to his wife's continuing concern in the bank after the birth of their first child in 1805. Of course, it is possible that Christiana welcomed her husband's interference and was glad to return to a life of caring for small children after her earlier introduction to the delights and tribulations of such a role in caring for her little half-brother. However, her father's confidence in her ability to take charge of his bank does suggest a keen interest in work outside her home, a character trait clearly disapproved of by her husband.

The bank continued as Dixon and Dalton for many years, until early in 1844 when the town was passing through an unparalleled depression, with no fewer than sixty blast furnaces being shut down. The bank had to suspend payment, though it was considered that there was a good likelihood of their paying in full.

Christiana died on New Year's Day 1840 and was buried later that week in Broome church. Her memorial appears in the Wolverhampton Chronicle of the 8 January 1840. It was perhaps fortunate that she did not live to see the disaster that was so soon to destroy her family bank, which, having been bereft of her partnership by her husband's intervention, she would have been powerless to avoid.

HANNAH SWAINE, wife with brothers. Hannah Swaine joined her three brothers in their long standing wool combing business in Halifax. Robert, John and Edward Swaine owned woollen mills in Copley, Haley Hill and Bradford as well as the Halifax Commercial Bank. The Swaines were the oldest Presbyterian family in Bradford; Miles Swayne of Horton, dying in 1515, had been buried in the church of St Peter and St Paul. Hannah's father, Joseph Swaine, 1703-1787, also owned land and houses at Lower Burnet Field, Esholt Hawksworth and Manningham, though the bulk of his fortune came from his worsted mills.

Hannah's mother was Bathshua, (*sic*) daughter of the Revd Robert Hesketh of Tingley, '*who traced her descent from the Lords Eure of Witton Castle, Durham and Stokesley Manor, Cleveland.*' Hannah was born in 1751 and married her first cousin Samuel, 1750-1789, son of William Swaine, her father's younger brother. Samuel does not appear to have taken any part in the family businesses, neither the wool trade nor the bank. They had one son, Robert. Samuel's early death meant that Hannah had been a widow for fifty-two years when she died, aged ninety, in 1841.

Hannah, was named as a partner in the family bank in 1803, at which date a panic brought on by the discovery of fraud by an official in the Bank of England had caused a country-wide run on local banks. Both banks in Halifax were affected, but survived through the support of their customers who signed a declaration of confidence. However, four years later, in July of 1807, the creditors of Bros Swaine & Co were invited to attend a meeting to discuss the situation of the bank, affected by the general trade depression. It was a tribute to the integrity of the bank that a resolution was passed to allow the partners to arrange the closure of the business. Advertisements in the local papers during the subsequent autumn declaring that the notes of the bank remained valid show the continuing public confidence in the Swaine bank. The estate paid at least three dividends though Robert Swaine's large mansion had to be sold. Nevertheless, by 1810 the family could no longer avoid failure in their wool business and were declared bankrupt.

In spite of this disaster, the next generation of Swaines appear to have recovered their fortunes, remaining prominent and landowning citizens. Hannah's youngest brother, Edward, had enjoyed a successful business career in London, where he was also active in promoting legislation to benefit the wool industry. From London he moved to Leipzig and Weimar where he died in 1837 aged eighty. His descendants included army officers and a physician attending the Duchess of Kent, the mother of Queen Victoria.

JANE ST AUBYN, widow with cousin. Jane was descended from an old Cornish family; her grandfather was William Arundell of Tolverne and her father, Robert Arundell of Helston was a surgeon in the Royal Navy who continued his career as Collector of Customs at Falmouth. During the 1760s Jane's life in her father's home at Helston was spent in a neighbourhood within which many branches of the St Aubyn family had their houses. They and the Arundells had already intermarried in previous generations and Jane would have known in childhood both her future husband and John St Aubyn, the 5th baronet, whose bank she was later to join. Their circle may well also have included the Bassetts of Teludy, near Penryn, banker of Truro. Members of this family, Royalists in the Civil Wars, had sold St Michael's Mount to the St Aubyns a couple of generations back. The family of Catherine and Catherine Payton Fox lived at Perranarworthal, very near to Clowance, the St Aubyn's house, so an enclave of banking families, some with women partners, surrounded Jane as she grew up.

Jane married Francis St Aubyn of Collin Mixton in 1774 and they made their home at Stoke Dameral, where their daughter Jane was born. She married back into the Scottish branch of her mother's family, the Arundells of Ben-Jarg, Dumfriesshire and had nine children. Francis St Aubyn died at Stoke Damerel in 1810. He had never been interested in business or public affairs, unlike his grandfather, Francis St Aubyn of St Michael's Mount, younger brother of the 1st baronet, who had been a barrister and mayor of Marazion in 1684. Another entrepreneurial St Aubyn, the 5th baronet, was a founder partner of the Devonport bank by 1790. The bank was built on land acquired by this somewhat eccentric family through the marriage of his father, the 4th Bart to Catherine Morice, an heiress whose dowry included the manor of Stoke Damerel on which the docks were built, together with a fortune of £10,000, amassed, oddly, in half-crowns, so that a cart was needed to bring it to her new home. Their son John succeeded his father as 5th Bart when only fourteen, and was sent away to Westminster school. When still in his early twenties he began a colourful career by installing his first mistress, Martha Nicholls, the beautiful daughter of a successful landscape gardener, at his elegant house Clowance. Five children were born of this union between 1783 and 1790. Sir John continued to support Martha and the children even after taking another mistress, Julia Vinnicombe, who bore him their first child in 1790. He met her when she was only a child and was so delighted with her cleverness that he sent her to be educated in Cheltenham. He treated these ladies so generously as to escape social disapproval: indeed, it was said of him that *'he has had in succession two Cornish women to live with him, both persons of good conduct in every other respect. All the children he educated as he would have done legitimate sons and daughters and the marriage portions of fifteen children amounted to £130,000.'* All Julia's ten children were born before Sir John eventually married her in 1822. Julia too was a lovely woman, and both she and Martha were painted by Opie, of whom Sir John was a friend and patron. He combined this unconventional behaviour with becoming High Sheriff of Cornwall when he was twenty-three, and MP for Penryn and Helston from 1807 till 1812. He was a prominent freemason and Provincial Grand Master of his Lodge for fifty-four years, as well as being an FSA, a Fellow of the Linnean Society and of the Royal Society. In 1804 he started a mineralogical collection, a field in which Elizabeth Carne, another Cornish banker (cf *p. 153*), later worked with her father. A man with such enlightened views on contemporary society would not hesitate to bring a woman partner into his business so when John St Aubyn wished to enlarge the partnership of the Plymouth Dock Bank, it was not altogether surprising that he should invite the cousin whom he had known since childhood, to join him in 1810. Recently widowed, Jane would have been able to give her whole attention to the bank, her home at Stoke Damerel being fortunately so close to it. She justified his confidence by taking over as senior partner on his retirement, with Charles Carpenter of

Moditonham, Thomas Clinton Shiells of East Stonehouse and Henry Incledon Johns. When Jane, together with Charles Carpenter, retired in 1818 from their successful bank, it was carried on by the two latter partners, who failed in 1825, a disastrous year for business.

Fortunately for Jane St Aubyn, long before this failure, she had moved to Portman Place in London where she lived comfortably having inherited her Arundell family estates. Although successful in business, Jane St Aubyn was unfortunate in outliving her husband and children, and three of her nine grandchildren. The six survivors, by then in the guardianship of an uncle on their late father's side, are named in her will.

ELIZABETH RUNDLE, widow with father and brother. In the neighbouring town of Tavistock Elizabeth Rundle was a partner in a family bank at much the same date as Jane St Aubyn. Her family could be described as *'minor gentry'* but were also active in trade as brewers and grocers. Elizabeth's father was John Gill of Tavistock who had married on the 3 February 1754 Prothesia Edgecombe of Milton Abbot. Elizabeth was born in 1758 and at her baptism her father was named as *'of Roman's Lee,'* (or Leigh), a holding of Tavistock Abbey. He had inherited the house from his father Thomas who died there in 1765, his coffin being carried to his grave at Tavistock on the shoulders of eight doughty grandsons. On her mother's side Elizabeth's grandfather was Richard Edgecombe, gentleman, of Milton Abbot, and her uncle, the Revd Edgecombe, was rector of Sydenham Damerel from 1780 until his death in 1795. On 19 April 1786 he officiated at the marriage of his niece Elizabeth to William Rundle, grocer, of Tavistock. Their first child, William, was born in 1787 followed by seven more children, of whom three died young and five survived her.

The family bank, Gill & Co was first listed in 1791. It does not seem that William Rundle was ever connected with the bank although he was in partnership with the Gill family as grocers and brewers in 1797. At his death in 1804 William's will shows that he had originally left Elizabeth capital which she would forfeit were she to marry again, but that he had very soon added a codicil allowing her the use of the income from that capital even if she remarried. Clearly, though he disliked the idea of a future husband gaining control of the fortune he had himself worked so hard to amass, he was confident that his widow, in sole control, would be capable of using it to the best advantage. By 1810, still a widow in control of her own money, Elizabeth had joined her father and brother as a partner in the bank.

In 1812 and 1813 the partnership also included her nephew John Hornbrook Gill and a member of the Bray family who had at one time been business associates of the Gills. Elizabeth died aged sixty on 25 July 1818, having retired from the bank three months previously. At that date the property she owned included houses in Launceston, one near the church and the other in the fishmarket, and her will mentions her daughters, Elizabeth and Grace, still unmarried, and her sons William, John and Nicholas. Her father John Gill survived her but chose to retire from the bank and his other business interests when the bank partnership was re-formed in 1820. John and Nicholas, Elizabeth's sons, replaced him in the bank, joining their cousin John Hornbrook Gill.

In July of the following year, Nicholas married Anne, only daughter of William Harris Harness, a surgeon. The eldest brother, William, took over their grandfather's grocery business. John not only joined in the grocery as well as the bank partnership but made a prudent marriage to his cousin Barbara Gill and went on to become MP for Tavistock from 1835 to 1843. He was still listed as a bank partner in 1834, perhaps continuing until his death in 1864 in Hampstead, where he is buried. Nicholas last appeared in the partnership in 1830 but lived on until 1872, dying at the respectable age of 87 and is buried close to Tavistock, at Sydenham Damerel. Nearly a hundred years after the bank opened a member of Elizabeth's family Richard Butler Edgecombe Gill was a partner when in 1889 it was absorbed by Fox, Fowler & Co, which later became part of Lloyds Bank.

MARY SIMMONDS, widow with brother-in-law and nephews. Mary Wilkes was brought up in the world of industry and commerce. She was an active woman who held partnerships in cotton spinning and manufacturing with various partners at Manchester, Ashby de la Zouche, Measham and Appleby. Her father, Joseph Wilkes, was born at Overseal in Derbyshire in 1732, where he was in business with his brothers, but had branched out in his forties. In 1775 he joined in partnership in cotton spinning at Tamworth with the Peel family, made famous later by the Prime Minister, Sir Robert Peel. He prospered, and by 1780 was able to buy the manor of Measham near Ashby, where he set up a cotton mill and started a coal mine. In 1780 he also opened two banks, one at Burton and the other at Ashby, the first in Leicestershire outside the county town. Ten years later, in 1790, his entrepreneurial spirit found another outlet when in partnership with the Peels, he founded a bank in London, at 33 Poultry. Even after the Peels withdrew from this bank the cotton spinning and calico manufacture were continued by the Wilkes/Peel partnership until its dissolution in 1800.

Another of Joseph Wilkes's business interests was the canal from Ashby to Nuneaton, which was slower to show a profit. During his lifetime the canal company, as so often occurs, found the expenses had been under-estimated, and the amount of coal to be carried over-estimated, and had to contend with complaints from a good customer, Pickfords, about lock charges, as well as competition from the Trent and Mersey Canal Company, so that no dividend was paid until 1828. Local agriculture was yet another of his wide-ranging interests, involving him as a supporter of Robert Bakewell, the famous Leicestershire sheep breeder.

Comfortably off, Mary Wilkes grew up in Measham Manor where hard work and money making were the accepted way of life. After her father's death—amazingly, intestate—in 1805 she apparently considered business as her future career. She married John Simmonds, an engineer and canal tunneller who may well have been an associate of her father's in the Nuneaton canal system. Their first child was born in 1799 and was named after her father Joseph Wilkes Simmonds. John Simmonds had died before 1812, also intestate, his wife Mary named as being administrator. The name John Simmonds does not ever appear in the bank partnership. Mary is named as a partner at Ashby and Burton in 1812, 1813 and 1830, and the surname Simmonds appeared in 1810 and 1831 so it is probable that she was a partner over the whole period.

The bank issued its own notes at both Ashby and Measham, adding extra work as well as greater business opportunities, and with some twenty years in this partnership at Ashby, Burton and Measham as well as her interests in the cotton business at Manchester, Mary was by no means the least industrious of women bankers. The banks in which Mary was a partner, grouped round Ashby de la Zouche were very much a family concern, indeed, in 1805 all the partners were related to her by birth or marriage, including her brother-in-law Thomas Fisher of Castle Donnington, and his sons, Thomas and John, who were still with her in the bank in 1830, together with Edward Mammett, previously a clerk in the bank, who had also been in the engineering partnership with her husband until it was dissolved in 1804. In 1831 the bank is still listed in a local guide as Fisher, Simmonds and Mammett, but after this, there is some discrepancy between two accounts of its fate. One source declares that the bank had always been insolvent and '*failed for £80,000.*' Another account gives a happier ending, telling us that the '*bank maintained a strong business, surviving storms and stresses*' but that by 1834, when many private country banks were being taken over by joint stock companies the partners were ready to accept an offer of absorption from the Leicestershire Banking Company.

Although Ashby was only twenty miles from headquarters in Leicester, the rumour that legislation would impose some geographical limitation on the scope of joint stock banking caused some delay. In 1835, on the death of Edward Mammett, the bank's business was temporarily suspended, as was often necessary while the affairs of the deceased were wound up. The joint stock company immediately opened a branch at Ashby, appointing the senior clerk of the private bank as manager, and buying their premises and goodwill for £3,500.

ELIZABETH BRADLEY, widow with uncle and aunt-in-law; **KATHERINE HARVEY**, widow with niece-in-law. Two women, Elizabeth Catherine Bradley (sometimes spelt Bradly), and her aunt by marriage, Katherine Harvey partners in the Sandwich bank, were both members of prominent Kentish families.

Elizabeth was born 16 July 1749, the daughter of Margaret, born Harvey, and Thomas Freeman. She married in 1773 William Wyborn Bradley. She lived to be seventy-one, dying in 1820 after a life of considerable business achievement. Her mother's family were successful citizens in many walks of life, in banking and brewing and also in providing Admirals of the Fleet. It was Elizabeth's uncle Samuel Harvey, a brewer and maltster, who founded the Sandwich bank in 1796. Elizabeth joined him as a partner in the brewery and in the bank by 1810, by which time she had been a widow for some ten years, and her children were grown up. She became senior partner in the bank on her uncle's death in 1813 when his widow Catherine, an executor of his will, became a partner in the bank, but junior to his niece Elizabeth. At that date it was more usual for a senior bank partner to leave his widow the seniority. The difference here reflects Samuel's high opinion of his niece after years of successful business partnership in both brewing and banking and she was seven years older than her aunt-in-law, Catherine.

Elizabeth's husband, William Wyborne Bradley, was the scion of another brewing family. Her husband's maternal grandfather, William Wyborne, had been a prosperous brewer, owning many public houses and other property in Sandwich. His will, proved in April 1764, showed him to have owned the Green Dragon, the Garden Kings, Crispin, the Ship, the Black Bear and the Bull as well as two breweries and the brew house at his own house. He left an income to his wife and his brothers and sister. His cousin Mary Kingsford was to continue to '*manage the yeast*' for his daughter Mary Bradley '*as she had done for him*,' living in the same house as his daughter and her children, with free board and lodging. All this property was to descend to his grandchildren, William Wyborne Bradley (Elizabeth's future husband) and Stephen Bradley.

In their turn, William and Elizabeth called their two sons William Wyborne and Stephen. When Elizabeth Bradley retired from the bank in 1815 her son William took her place for a year, after a successful career in local politics. He had been elected mayor in 1805 and his brother Stephen, much younger, followed him in the office four times between 1817 and 1834; clearly a family with a strong sense of civic responsibility.

William and Elizabeth's daughter Elizabeth married her cousin Sir John Harvey, KCB, one of the Harvey's admirals. The Harveys were a close-knit family, frequently inter-marrying among themselves and their bank partners' families. For instance, several marriages were made into the family of Henry Matson, one of the earliest partners in the bank. Revd Richard Harvey, Fellow of All Souls' College, Oxford and vicar of Eastrey was Elizabeth Bradley's uncle and Katherine Harvey's brother-in-law and married Judith, daughter of Charles Matson of Wingham Court. Their son Richard, who succeeded as vicar of Eastrey, continued the family tradition in the bank as well, joining as partner and executor of his uncle Samuel Harvey's will.

Elizabeth's aunt, Mary Roberta Harvey, married John Matson, Town Clerk of Sandwich and Chief Justice of Bahama, an island in the West Indies, another relation of Henry Matson. In addition to this web of intermarriage, the Bradleys had connections with a woman banker in Wales. Catherine Wyborne, youngest sister and co-heir of John Wyborne of Hawkwell Place, Kent, married Phillip Jones of Llanarth and Upton Park, Berkshire. Their son John, banker in Abergavenny, left his partnership to his widow, Catherine's daughter-in-law, Mary.

Samuel Harvey had doubtless caused a sensation when, in 1773, the year of his niece's marriage, he eloped to Gretna Green with the seventeen-year-old Catherine, daughter of Robert Maundy, a timber merchant. There is no information as to the reason for this aberrant behaviour, but she was ten years younger than her husband and may have wanted a romantic spice to the marriage. Be that as it may, Catherine soon settled down to the accepted routine of married life. Their first son William Maundy was born in 1774 the year after the elopement, and she bore five more children during the next twelve years, two boys and three girls, of whom only two of the latter survived their tenth birthday. The fact that Catherine and Samuel gave two of their sons the additional name of Maundy after their maternal grandfather, suggests that it was not the disapproval of Catherine's family that caused the elopement. Two months before Samuel died in August 1813, he and Catherine had had the sad news of the death at sea of their eldest and only surviving son William; himself a widower, he left a young son, also called William Maundy. In this disastrous year, Catherine must have relied on the support of her two surviving daughters, Elizabeth and Mary, both by then married. After Samuel's death Catherine succeeded to his partnership which she held until the bank was dissolved in 1815 when she and Mrs Elizabeth Catherine Bradley retired. Catherine lived on until November 1835, dying in her eightieth year.

The Sandwich bank, after the retirement of the last of the Harvey / Bradley partners in 1816, was carried on by the Emerson and Hodgson families. It survived until 1842 and closed without failure, still a private partnership after a period when very many banks became joint stock companies.

ANN HOWARD, wife with brother-in-law. Ann Weedon was married in 1778 to John Howard. She was still a minor, only eighteen, while John was thirty-six. They had eight children in the next twenty years, the last child being born in 1800. The Howard family owned considerable estates, though they and their connections were substantial tradesmen, brewers, bakers and corn-chandlers.

The Rickmansworth bank is first mentioned in 1809 as Howard & Co, probably founded by Simeon Howard who is listed as senior partner in 1812, with Ann Howard and Henry Plaistowe of Hyde Hall, who had married Simeon's daughter Sarah. When Simeon died in 1815 he left them his own house, Corner Hall, still standing (in 2000), a handsome half-timbered house in the Colne valley near the Uxbridge road. Ann's husband John Howard, Simeon's older brother, died in 1816 without his name having ever appeared in the partnership lists or having taken any interest in the bank. Nor did any of their sons or daughters join the family bank. It was Ann's own initiative that took her into partnership with her brother-in-law Simeon by 1812. The Rickmansworth bank issued its own promissory notes and by 1813 had added two names to the title under which their notes were licensed, two nephews of John and Simeon, Edward and Thomas Howard, who were still partners in 1820.

Ann died a year after her husband, in 1817 aged only fifty-eight. The bank was carried on by the 1820 partnership, strengthened by the addition of Henry Plaistowe's brother William, who joined the bank in 1821, adding ten thousand pounds to the capital. In spite of this, however, the bank foundered in the general panic of 1826, when William's distress was such that he died, as has been suggested, by his own hand. This was a later manifestation of the 1825 monetary crisis (*see Chapter 9 and Conclusions*).

CATHERINE FOX, widow with son, daughter and nephew. Catherine Fox banker was obliged, to accept at an even earlier age than Elizabeth Evans of Derby the responsibility for her younger brothers and sisters. She was only ten years old when her mother died and she took charge of her father and his household for nearly twenty years. Catherine was the daughter of William Young Esq of Leominster, and Hannah Payton. She was co-heir to her uncle James Payton, a Quaker, and a friend of the Darby family at Coalbrookdale. He lived in Dudley, at the same date as, and perhaps acquainted with William Amphlett, Christiana's grandfather.

Catherine was twenty-nine when in 1780 she married George Croker Fox II, a year younger than herself. They built Grove Hill, a fine house which their son, George Croker Fox III inherited on his father's death in 1807. Catherine had married into a solid mercantile family, a household name in the West Country. Her father-in-law, George Croker Fox I founded the firm of G C Fox and Co in Fowey in 1754 but moved with the firm to Falmouth in 1762. Entry into the Fox family brought Catherine many relationships in the banking world, mostly Quakers. Her father-in-law married Mary Were and was thus connected with the London bankers, Curtis, Were, Robarts and Co. Fox cousins were bankers at Wellington in Somerset and both families were connected with other noted Quaker bankers, the Lloyds and the Barclays. Family marriages also connected them with Tregelles partners in the Fox bank at Falmouth and with bankers at Kingsbridge, Plymouth, Ipswich, Bristol, Kendal and Manchester.

Through another marriage, this one outside the Society of Friends, this prudent family connected themselves to the Smiths, bankers in London, and through them, to the earliest country bankers, the Smiths of Nottingham, Hull etc. There were also banking connections in Catherine's own family such as through her aunt, with the Bevan clan, bankers throughout East Anglia and at Brighton. Close ties with other women bankers came from the friendship between Catherine's cousin, Catherine Payton, and the Darby women bankers of Coalbrookdale. A more tenuous link with another woman banker was through the friendship of her cousin Charles of Trebah and Tredrea and his wife with Samuel Taylor Coleridge. He would surely have spoken to them of his great admiration of Elizabeth Evans, banker at Derby.

It was not only Catherine and her husband who invested in bricks and mortar, for much of the family wealth was devoted to building houses in and around Falmouth providing mutual support between members of the family. In 1788 Robert Were Fox I built Bank House, named for the ridge on which it stood and his son, Robert Were Fox II built Rose Hill, though he later moved to Bank House which he inherited from his father. Other notable houses built by the Fox family include Penjerrick, Glendurgen and Trebah, all with equally fine gardens. Living in houses close together, the family depended on each other for company and mutual support.

Many entries in Barclay Fox's Journal, especially those concerning the house on the Bank, illustrate this closeness, such as *'after the marriage we adjourned to the Bank for cake;' 'we drank tea at the Bank,' 'when I went to the Bank I found the doctor was with grandmamma.'* Other medical emergencies were shared, as when *'Sampson entered the office aghast and announced that Firefly's leg was broken. I went with him to the Bank stable.'* Happier times are recorded; *'we had a famous family dinner at the Bank. I do like the large Christmas assembling of kith and kin'* and *'quartered at Grove Hill by day and returned to Bank at night.'* So the Alexanders at Goldrood were not the only Quaker family to make Christmas into a festive occasion.

A Cornish historian, R M Fitzmaurice, questioned whether G C Fox & Co ever included banking in their business because they are not listed as bankers in a Falmouth Directory of 1815. This omission, however, can be explained by the entry in Leekey's 1813 Stamp Office list of *'Country Bankers, containing all the Banking Companies in England and Wales who issue Promissory Notes payable on demand.'* In this list G C Fox appears, not in Falmouth but at Perran Wharf. Perranarworthal, as it is spelt on a modern map, lies on the main road, half way between Falmouth and Truro, and was also the site of G C Fox's engineering foundry. Charles Fox, a family historian, had no doubt that the business included banking, stating that *'at one time more faith was placed in a note from G C Fox's bank than in a note from any other bank in Falmouth.'* Before he died in 1807, George Croker Fox, Catherine's husband, may well have discussed with her the possibility of founding the bank which first appeared in 1808. As he did not bequeath the senior partnership to her, but left the family to make their own arrangements, she is not included as a widow inheriting the bank from her husband. The name of George Croker Fox which heads the partnership in Leekey's 1813 list must be Catherine's son, third of that name. The partnership also includes Catherine, her daughter Catherine Payton Fox and her nephew Robert Were Fox.

CATHERINE PAYTON FOX, spinster with mother, brother and cousin. As the daughter of two bankers and connected as she was with so many banking families, the inclusion of her name in the bank partnership of 1813 can scarcely have occasioned much surprise. She was independent minded and expressed some pretty forthright opinions in her journal. She enjoyed visiting friends, including the Lloyds, Quaker bankers in Birmingham, and on one occasion while with them, met the Schimmelpennicks, whose daughter Marianne was to marry Thomas Tyndall, later inheriting his bank at Bristol.

Catherine was amused by the eccentricities of the people she met, writing while on a journey through Gloucestershire of the *'lovely seat of Sir Onesipherous Pearl, a queer name truly and from what we hear he is a queer man. Disappointed while young and therefore hating all women, has as few about him as he can, even including servants.'* She reflects that he is *'a crusty old bachelor, truly, for what woman would hate ALL men because disappointed in ONE.'* Her travels kept her in touch with modern advances, already arrived in London but still to reach provincial towns. On one visit to town Catherine came to hear of the velocipede, or bicycle, trial, which was a new machine not yet used in Falmouth.

After more than a decade in the bank, on holiday at Montreuil-sur-Mer, Catherine Payton Fox died there, aged thirty-four, of a seizure, in 1823. Her mother survived her, living to grieve for her daughter until her own death in 1829. Any attack on the admirable Quaker beneficence could only be made from within the Society itself. Barclay Fox noted in his journal of April 1842 a visit to Penjerrick of two Quaker ladies.

> *'The former'* he wrote, *'is all meekness and modesty and unconscious of what an unruly passion can possibly mean. She is quiet, amiable, inanimate, being appropriately clad in the most unpretending drapery of the order. The latter is a strong-minded, abrupt person, gifted with plain sense and sincerity, great conscientiousness as far as she sees, but unable to see good beyond the limits of her own shadow. She is one of the narrow school who virtually think self-denial IN ITSELF holy, and who cannot discern the inward principle except in the outward form in which they themselves have been educated.'*

Perhaps the Falmouth bankers better exemplified the Quakers described by Caroline Fox, not herself a banker, in a letter to her friend Elizabeth Carne, banker at Penzance, on 31 January 1855,

'*Why what a fuss we made about slave trade, then prisons,
refusal to swear, paid ministry. Quakers are the most difficult
and bizarre body in Christendom, but perhaps thy special
allusion is to our not vigorously opposing the money-getting
spirit of the age. Ah, my dear Elizabeth, there is grievous
amount of truth in this (supposed) charge, but I will say it
is IN SPITE OF the earnest advice and beseeching of our
official superiors. I always try to account for the phenomenon
by remembering essentially a middle class community, that
amongst us industry, perseverance and energy are habitually
cultivated, and that as our crotchets keep us out of almost
all the higher walks of professional life, this industry,
perseverance and energy is found in the money market and
is apt to succeed therein. All I can say in apology (for it does
require an apology) is that the wealth we gain is not generally
spent on ourselves alone.*'

Caroline Fox had plenty of opportunity to judge the veracity of
all this at first hand from two Quaker women relations, partners in
the family bank at Falmouth. Caroline's suggestions to Elizabeth as
to the charitable use of money acquired in trade was certainly not lost
on her. There was nothing priggish nor limited about the Fox family
giving, for the wealth they amassed through their various enterprises
was focussed on the sea and on education. They gave to such good
causes as the Cornwall Seamen's Benevolent Trust, the Royal National
Lifeboat Institution, Ship-wrecked Mariners, and Missions to Seamen.
They supported the Falmouth Maritime Museum and founded one of
the earliest polytechnic societies in the country, in order to promote
education in the arts and sciences, especially among the under-
privileged.

ELIZABETH CATHERINE THOMAS CARNE, Spinster with nephews. '*How
momentous and fruitful is the truth*' Caroline Fox wrote in the letter quoted
earlier. She added that '*It may be hidden yet still living in that form of religion
which you profess.*' Caroline's phrase only grudgingly concedes validity to
the Wesleyan beliefs strongly held by Elizabeth and her family. Indeed,
her father, Joseph Carne was said to be consulted by every Wesleyan
chapel in Cornwall.

Caroline Fox's belief that Quakers had so few outlets and yet were so hard-working that they were bound to make money, in spite of their simple tastes, was exemplified also in the non-conformist Carne family. William Carne, Elizabeth's grandfather, was one of the founders of the Penzance bank of Batten, Carne & Oxnam in 1795, continuing as a partner until his death in 1836 at the age of eighty-two. Like many other Penzance bankers the partners were also merchants and ship-owners. His son Joseph was born at Truro in 1782 and educated at the Wesleyan school in Keynsham, where the great brass foundry belonged to Richard Champion, Quaker banker at Bristol.

In 1808 Joseph Carne married Mary Thomas, daughter of William Thomas MD of Kidwelly, near Haverfordwest. After living for some time in Penzance they moved to Riviere House in Phillack when he was appointed to manage Sandys, Carne and Vivian, the Cornish Copper Company's smelting works at Hayle. Joseph Carne was a professional geologist, many years Treasurer of the Cornish Geological Society, author of many works on the subject and was elected Fellow of the Royal Society in 1818. He later became an honorary member of the Cambridge Philosophical Society.

Joseph's children were all born in Phillack, first two sons, both of whom died relatively young, one leaving a daughter. Joseph and his wife left four daughters, the youngest of whom was Elizabeth, born in 1817. She was a precocious child, admired at school for her prowess in mathematics, classics and modern languages as well as her interest in political economy. Later her scholarly concentration on geology, as keen as her father's, led to the submission of papers to the Transactions of the Royal Geological Society of Cornwall. These included '*Cliff Boulders and the Former Condition of the land and sea in the Land's End district*', '*The Age of the Maritime Alps surrounding Mentone*'; '*On the Transition and Metamorphosis of Rocks*' and '*On the Nature of Forces that have acted in the Formation of the Land's End Granite.*' She also contributed many articles to the *London quarterly review*.

Between 1859 and 1871 Elizabeth published four books, the first, under the pseudonym of John Altroyd Witterly, *Three Months Rest at Pau in the Winter and Spring of 1859*. She published *England's Three Wants* anonymously in 1871 and two under her own name, *Country Towns and the Place they fill in Modern Civilization* in 1868, and *The Realm of*

Truth in 1873, the year she died, an expression of her early interest in political economy. She busied herself in many aspects of the life of her local community, establishing the Mineralogical Museum of the Royal Geological Society as well as a museum open to the public to display her father's valuable collection of minerals. Perhaps more gratefully appreciated, Elizabeth founded schools at Wesley Rock, Carfury and Bosullow, small villages near Penzance which might not otherwise have had any school. Very practically, Elizabeth kept Penzance rates down by avoiding the necessity for a School Board by ensuring that there was adequate school accommodation.

Although strictly speaking a Wesleyan, she was ecumenical in her giving and provided a ring of bells for St Mary's parish church. In spite of her earlier agreement with Caroline Fox on the ill-directed zeal of some missionaries, she also gave generously to their efforts overseas. She was noted for her discriminating generosity to the poor and her hatred of having her kindness known. Like other women bankers in coastal towns, such as Margaret Campion in Whitby and Sarah Rice in Dover, Elizabeth Carne owned a fleet of ships and used them in successful mercantile trading. A wealthy woman, she well knew how to make and manage her money. She took on the responsibilities of the senior partnership in the bank on her father's death in 1858 and continued as such until her own death in September 1873.

She died of a 'low fever' of only six weeks, remaining active almost until the last It proved fortunate for the continuance of the family bank that, as Elizabeth remained single, her elder sister Mary married. Her husband, Archibald Colquhoun Ross, was a medical doctor in Funchal where their first child, Archibald, was born in 1843. Funchal remained their home until her husband's death in 1856. Young Archibald was sent home to attend the Grammar School in Penzance, where he presumably lived with his aunt Elizabeth and his grandfather until later he was sent to Brighton College. In 1862 he returned to Cornwall as an Ensign in the Penzance Rifles, and that year he also began work at the bank in Penzance, taking additionally the name of Carne. Sadly, he died two years later, aged only twenty-one. His younger brother Charles Campbell Carne Ross was born in London in 1849 and was educated at Brighton College and Trinity College Cambridge.

Charles, a public-spirited young man, was five times mayor of Penzance between 1877 and 1882 as well as being elected MP for St Ives from 1881 to 1885. Charles made a suitable marriage in 1870 with Isabel Emily, the widow of his mother's cousin Revd John Carne who had died in 1868 and daughter of Edward Holland Esq of Canada, Commissary General. In 1872 Charles became a partner in the bank, taking his aunt's senior partnership on her death a year later.

This remarkable family traded successfully in a private partnership bank from 1795 when William Carne was one of the founders through the entry of his son Joseph in 1813 and his granddaughter Elizabeth in 1858. Finally, his great-grandson Charles entered the bank, introducing the fourth generation of the family. Although their last listing as a private bank had been as Bodilly & Ross, the joint stock company which the private partnership formed in 1890 returned to the old name of Batten, Carne & Carne. Thus the name of Carne which first appeared over William's bank in 1795, was last seen one-hundred-and-one years later, when in 1896 they were absorbed into the larger local joint stock bank, Bolitho's, who in turn became part of Barclays Bank in 1905.

The eleven women discussed in this chapter show the family nature of these private partnership banks as well as the adaptability of women to varied circumstances. The three women who entered banks as spinsters, Christiana Amphlett, Elizabeth Carne, and Catherine Payton Fox, illustrate the vicissitudes of a banking career. Catherine Payton Fox was a young woman of twenty-four when she was made a partner with her mother, her brother and her cousin, a career sadly cut short by her early death of a seizure in Montreuil-sur-Mer aged thirty-four. These three, and the other unmarried women bankers, showed their contemporaries that it was possible for a single woman to enjoy some other career than that of a governess, while the intervention of Edward Dudley underlines the total authority of a husband at this period.

Chapter Five

Widows inheriting banks from their husbands

London: **AGATHA CHILD**, *London*; **CHARLOTTE MATTHEWS**, *London*.
Berkshire: **CATHERINE MARSH**, *Reading*; **LUCY DEAN**, *Reading*.
Hampshire: **ANN DOWDEN**, *Alton*; **CAROLINE GUNNER**, *Bishop's Waltham*;
CAROLINE MARY ST BARBE, *Lymington*.
Kent: **SARAH RICE**, *Dover*; **ELEANOR MARY DOORNE**, *Rochester*.
Surrey: **ELIZABETH LA COST**, *Chertsey*.
Sussex: **LEONORA TILDEN SAMPSON**, *Hastings*.

London:

AGATHA CHILD. Agatha Edgar was the daughter of Mileson Edgar, of the Red House, Suffolk, and Alice Shaw, sole heir of her father William Shaw Esq of St Clements, Ipswich. The Edgar family had been landowners in Suffolk since the time of Henry VIII. Agatha's brother, also Mileson, married into another Suffolk family, the D'Eyes of Eye.

A girl from this land-owning background seems an unlikely candidate for the position of the first woman banker. Agatha married in 1730 Samuel Child, senior partner of the famous bank in London. The ancient house of Child's had its origin in William Wheeler's goldsmith's shop in the Chepe and as a pike-man, in July 1559, it is said that he had the honour of bowing to Queen Elizabeth as she rode through the City on her way to Greenwich. Francis Child, the son of Robert Child of Headington, Wiltshire, was apprenticed to Wheeler, after which his career followed the time-honoured course; the industrious apprentice marrying his master's daughter. Wheeler took his brother-in-law, Blanchard, into partnership and by 1672, after Wheeler's death, the firm became Blanchard and Child, at the sign of ye Marygold at Temple Bar. Francis Child, by keeping running cashes (current accounts) for his customers made a move towards becoming a banker as well as a goldsmith. At Blanchard's death in 1681 Francis Child inherited the business, together with the fortunes of both his late partners. This inheritance gave him solid backing for his move, at that date towards more specialized banking. The City viewed the change with suspicion, reflected in a pamphlet of 1676, entitled *The Mystery of the New-fashioned Goldsmiths or Bankers their Rise, Growth, State and Decay, Discovered in a Merchants Letter to a Country Gent who Desired to Bind his Son Apprentice to a Goldsmith.* This ridicules, not very subtly, the new trade.

Despite this resistance to the very idea of the 'new bankers' Childs bank flourished, having on its books many famous and some notorious clients. At one time or another Childs did business for customers as varied as Titus Oates, Barbara Villiers, Sarah Churchill, Lady Mary Wortley Montague and in 1687 Eleanor (Nell) Gwynne, who, in spite of her august patron, died in debt to the bank. Fortunately other customers were in better financial circumstances; during the later part of the eighteenth century, the payment of the Russell family's rents, for instance, being paid into Child's bank, with considerable advantage to their turnover.

Clients had their individual preferences which the bank needed to respect. At the time of the flotation of shares in the Bank of England the 1st Duke of Leeds wrote, somewhat flustered on 25 June 1694 to Sir Francis Child:

> '*Sire, I am informed that the subscription to the Bank do fill so fast that there is at this day near seven hundred thousand pounds subscribed, so that it must now necessarily be a bank. I therefore desire that you will subscribe £4,000 for me and pay in one thousand pounds, on my account, as the Act directs.*'

Duties as keepers of land-owners' rents had to be adapted to the client's needs. In 1713 the Earl of Lichfield wanted the bank to continue sending him letters with a note of the amount of his rents. On the other hand, Lady Carteret preferred a passbook, writing '*I shall be glad of a book as I used to have at Mr Meads with an account of all you have received upon this article.'* In spite of their best efforts, banks were not always able to keep their clients, as when the Oxford Canal Company transferred their business in 1795 from Child's to the Oxford bank of Fletcher & Parsons. Nor was it unknown for provincial clients to transfer accounts from one bank to another at frequent intervals to maximize the profits to themselves.

Not only did his bank do well, but Francis Child also prospered personally. He was successively alderman, then sheriff, was knighted by 1689 and became Lord Mayor in 1698. He was elected MP first for Devizes in several parliaments and was one of four MPs for the City in the first parliament called by Queen Anne in 1702. In that year too, using his increasing wealth to acquire property, he bought 42 Lincoln's Inn Fields (in 2010 part of the Royal College of Surgeons). He used this house to store his Rubens and his other *"sixty-seven works of art."* Shortly before his death in 1713 it was he who completed the purchase of Osterley Park, which became the family home.

Francis I was succeeded in the bank by three of his surviving sons, Robert also knighted, and also an MP, who died unmarried in 1721. His successor in the bank was his brother Francis. Francis II, also an innovator, introduced printed promissory notes in 1729, worded in the same way as those of the Bank of England. Like his father, he became Lord Mayor of London and was knighted in 1732. With interests that went outside the City, he represented Middlesex in parliament in 1721. Francis died in 1740 when his younger brother Samuel became head of the bank. By 1767 they had bought 38 Berkeley Square from the Duke of Manchester and employed Robert Adam and John Linnell to complete the interior decoration and furnishings. During the times when he and Agatha his wife were able to stay at Osterley, she especially must have been delighted to move with their sons to the country. They kept a pack of hounds and enjoyed a thorough-going country house way of life, no doubt reminding her of her Suffolk childhood. Nevertheless, when the necessity arose on her husband's death in 1752, Agatha proved herself perfectly capable of taking over his partnership.

The bank Agatha now managed seems an equally unlikely base for the entry of a woman into the City of London. A bank historian has reproduced a painting showing the building which housed the bank in 1750, as Agatha knew it. A red brick house stands tall, but is still dwarfed by the great stone arch of Temple Bar beside it. Child's Bank, it is said, was able to store records in the room over the gatehouse, though this does not look easy of access in the illustration. The bank is depicted again in 1879 when the Temple Bar was moved to Cheshunt. Once she had taken on the responsibility for the bank Agatha made her own decisions, confronting and peremptorily dismissing two apparently entrenched partners whose contribution she considered no longer adequate. She brought her two sons, Francis III and Robert II into the bank, but continued as head of the partnership until her death in 1763, when Francis also died, leaving Robert as senior partner of Francis Child Esq & Co.

After three centuries on the same site, at the sign of the Marygold, the name Child was kept on the sale of the bank to Glyn, Mills in 1924. This in turn was taken over by the Royal Bank of Scotland in 1939. Later this bank was involved in the merger which produced the National and Commercial Banking group in 1969.

CHARLOTTE MATTHEWS. Like many provincial industrialists Matthew Boulton of the Soho factory in Birmingham needed a banker in London to look after his interests there. For some years he relied on William Matthews to act for him and on William's death in 1791 he transferred his business to William's widow, *'the redoubtable Charlotte Matthews.'* She continued to act as his agent and banker as well as his monitor, lecturing him on his need for greater sobriety, a novel addition to the customary services of one's bankers. It was not until after she died in 1801 that the Birmingham factory set up its own agency in London.

Addendum. There are some indications of the existence of a sixth woman London banker, **SARAH GROVE**, a widow inheriting from her husband. In 1788 Leslie Grove and John Hood were in partnership as merchants in Crosby Square, London. In 1798 Leslie Grove was bankrupt at the same address as merchant and banker. A third reference names Sarah Grove, described as *' widow, of Taunton,'* in a bankruptcy commission with William Hood 'carrying on trade in Crosby Square, London' in 1816. It is possible to construct a scenario in which Leslie Grove and his partner John Hood, merchants, add banking to their trading during the ten years between 1788 and 1798 in Crosby Square, London, ending in disaster for Leslie Grove. The 1816 bankruptcy refers, possibly to the failure by Sarah, Leslie Grove's widow and her partner, William, heir of her husband's partner John Hood in their attempts to revive the business, following the death of one or both of the original partners. These entries, though suggestive, have not been considered strong enough to warrant the inclusion of Sarah Grove as a woman banker.

Berkshire:

CATHERINE MARSH, LUCY DEAN. Unfortunately, not every woman banker was successful. Two widows in Reading appear to have been as extravagant and unsuccessful as some male commentators apparently believed every woman banker to be. The bank which they inherited, however, was already in a parlous state, for the Reading bank of Marsh and Deane provides an unfortunately perfect example of how, in spite of apparently effective and well-off partners, a private bank partnership could most comprehensively fail. Sir Charles Marsh had a distinguished career in India during the war between 1756 and 1763 as an officer in the 84th Foot, from which he returned to Reading with an ample fortune. In 1765 he married Catherine, still not twenty-one, daughter of Samuel Case of Bath. She evidently persuaded her parents to join her in Reading, where she and her husband in due course put up a memorial to them in their parish church.

Charles and Catherine had five children, four sons and a daughter. Their two older sons joined the army in India but instead of making their fortune died there. Contrariwise, Henry, the fourth son made his way early, marrying, at eighteen, a rich widow. The third son William worked in the bank for a while before going up to Oxford in 1797 and took Holy Orders in 1800, becoming eventually a famous evangelical preacher. He served as curate at St Lawrence's Reading, until 1809, becoming also incumbent at Nettlebed and vicar of Basildon, Berkshire, where his three children were born, and from where he was able to take a filial interest in the family bank.

On his return from India with an ample fortune Charles Marsh interested himself in raising a regiment of volunteers in Berkshire, for which he received a knighthood in 1786. In 1788 he saw his total inexperience in business as no impediment to his furthering his prospects by opening the first Reading bank. He took as partner a younger man, Henry Deane, a member of a local brewing family. Henry had sold out his share in the brewery on his father's death and became a burgess with a comfortable income. He was elected mayor three times between 1782 and 1794.

The third founder of the bank, Eyre Evans Crowe, of Sindlesham Lodge, had served in India in the same regiment as Sir Charles. As they were all well-known figures in the town, they had no difficulty in attracting customers to their bank. The partners put in £1,000 each but allowed too many unsecured loans based on friendship or even acquaintance, and within a very few years the bank was fast piling up debts. Their situation cannot have been improved by the failure in 1790 of John Deane, a gambler cousin of Henry Deane. He had bought the Castle Brewery shares from Henry and banked with Marsh and Deane. He was Receiver General for Berkshire and followed the usual custom of leaving his tax receipts with the bank to extract the maximum interest before remitting them to London. On his bankruptcy the Receivership was divided between East and West Berkshire, and Henry Boyle Deane, Henry's elder son, succeeded to the post for the former, continuing the practice of leaving his receipts with the bank until the last moment.

Eyre Evans Crowe, the third partner, went bankrupt in 1798, the other two partners retaining his equity in the bank. Henry Deane died in 1799 leaving an estate of £10,000 which his son allowed to remain in the bank, though he did not become a partner at that date. Sir Charles Marsh, with no business acumen, was left as sole partner, failing to recognize that the bank was becoming more deeply indebted every year, so that the total debt at his death in 1805 had grown to £46,000. Some of the Marsh family appeared at this time to feel a keener sense of the real position of the bank. Early in 1805 Charles' son William discouraged Richard Westbrook, a successful grocer, from joining the partnership because of its debts, allowing morality to prevail over the expedience of support for his father's financial credit.

When Sir Charles died in August 1805, last of the three founders, the partnership was re-formed, with the two widows, Catherine Marsh and Lucy Deane as senior partners, the former contributing £3,000 and the latter £1,900. They were joined by Richard Westbrook who, disregarding William's advice, put in £3,000, and by Henry Boyle

Deane, whose equity was waived because he acted as managing partner and in consideration of the tax receipts deposited with the bank.

William Marsh, who had appeared so sensible of the dangers of debt before his father's death, now made a most egregious mistake. He had power of attorney for his mother, and foolishly paid into her account securities worth nearly £2,500, previously held in trust by Sir Charles as executor for a client, which Catherine, unaware of their provenance, drew out for her own use. When in 1811 it became necessary to settle with the beneficiaries, she had to take out a mortgage. She had also drawn out, little by little, more than another £5,000. It seems extraordinary that she had no idea of the risk she ran.

Her partner, Lucy Deane, though less extravagant, proved to have been imprudent at the very least, withdrawing some £700 of the £1,900 of her investment. On the other hand Lucy Deane clearly had a respect for an education from which, as a woman, she could not benefit. She sent her two sons, Henry Boyle and George, to be educated at Steventon by Revd George Austen, Jane Austen's father. They continued their education at St John's College, Oxford. George, the younger son, obtained a Doctorate of Civil Law in 1797, followed by a career in the church, and did not join the bank. Henry Boyle Deane graduated as MA in 1792. Poor Mrs Deane must have felt acute disappointment that her son Henry seemed to have profited little from his education, in respect of morality at least He showed great imprudence, if no worse, in his handling of the funds he raised as Receiver General. He proved unworthy of his trust by failing to remit sums to the Exchequer as they fell due, allowing them to be counted as part of the finances of the bank for longer than was legitimately acceptable. The amount thus owed had reached the indefensible sum of £30,000 by the date of the bankruptcy in 1815. Nor does the behaviour of the other partner, Richard Westbrook, indicate a greater level of financial or private responsibility. In his efforts to pay the tax due in 1811, he put into the bank not only his own money, but also the very considerable sum of £6,000 which he had borrowed from his maiden sisters, whom he thus involved in the disaster. The Reading bank failed in 1815 for £150,000, nearly half of which was unsecured. Catherine Marsh's estate yielded £1,460 and Lucy Deane's £1,890. They were fortunate in continuing to be granted a small personal allowance each, administered by the Commissioners.

When William Marsh had been presented to the living of St Peter's, Colchester, in 1814 he was joined there by his mother and his sister, Mary Maria Matilda, widow of Captain Bolton RN. His sister died that year and his mother Catherine probably did not return to Reading as she died in Colchester in 1824, aged eighty. Had she returned she would have been subjected to the opprobrium caused by the failure of the bank. Her monument in St Peter's commends her for being *'humble in prosperity, cheerful in adversity, Christian in her faith, immovable in her hope and abounding in charity.'* Having experienced the pain suffered by the whole family from the failure of their bank and feeling a measure of guilt from his own part in it, William Marsh saw his opportunity to make amends by preventing the failure of the Colchester bank of Crickitt, Round & Co by his timely action in 1825 by bringing in cash to support the bank. When the Reading bank failed in 1815 the resident partners were therefore Richard Westbrook, Lucy Deane and her son Henry Boyle Deane, on whom fell the brunt of the disaster. It is clear that the two women came into a bank which was already in a situation of terminal though unrecognized decline and cannot be held entirely responsible for the disaster. They failed, however, to reverse the financial mismanagement, indeed, increased it by their own personal imprudence.

Hampshire:

ANN DOWDEN. In the provincial town of Alton, in Hampshire, Ann Dowden took over her late husband's bank as well as his brewery in 1790. Since her husband's partner, James Baverstock, took the opportunity to leave Alton and move to Windsor, where his family were involved in banking and brewing, Ann co-opted William Lee as her partner. At this time Ann was described as *'widow, of Anstey'* and William Lee as *'gentleman.'* Anstey Park, Anstey Road and Anstey Lane are now part of the town of Alton, as is Dowden Grove, present reminders of a prosperous past The last mention of the bank is in a list of 1797 but William Lee carried on their brewery for some time longer, dissolving partnership with William Boyce as brewers and brandy merchants in 1812. Brewing remained one of the staple industries of the town, however, and for many years connoisseurs could enjoy Alton ales and stouts. Alton's other industry was the growing of watercress which was sent to London on 'the watercress line' until the 1960s. The line was abolished by Dr Beeching, and was until 2000 carried on as a 'Heritage line.'

CAROLINE GUNNER. Chronologically the next Hampshire widow to take over a bank was Caroline Gunner, the daughter of Edward Hale of Hambledon House, Hambledon. This handsome house stands in six or seven acres on a hill top overlooking the village, where the Bat and Ball public house commemorates the early days of cricket. Monuments in the church record the death of her father in 1870, of her mother Caroline who lived to be ninety, dying in 1897 and of her sisters Rose Agnes and Fanny. She married Charles James Gunner, a solicitor and banker of Bishop's Waltham, son of William Gunner who founded the bank there in 1809, and Lucy Matilda Ridge. The Ridge family were settled at Cheriton Manor, where Thomas Ridge was Master of Foxhounds, a famous pack which in former days the Prince Regent often followed and the hunt button still carries his insignia, the three feathers. The Prince's entourage was famous for its expensive living and its gambling, the pitfalls of which, surprisingly, these squirarchal families seem to have avoided. The three families, Ridge, Hale and Gunner, met every year hunting and at Hambledon House for the cricket season.

Caroline and Charles set up house in Holm Oak, Bank Street, Bishop's Waltham. The bank premises and their house were an integral building, with a connecting door upstairs to the solicitor's office and downstairs to the bank. A large steel safe for customers' money stood in the cellar, which was reached from a trap door in Holm Oak, concealed by a carpet and a large table, moved morning and evening to put away the money. The bank was opened on the 11th October 1809 by Thomas Fox, (1765–1834), Stephen Steele, (1763–1823), John Golding Seymour, (1773–1840) and William Gunner, (1777–1857).

Thomas Fox and his brother in London were wine merchants, the latter taking care of the country bank's contacts there. The partners included an unusual mixture for Stephen Steele was a local farmer, John Goulding Seymour a doctor and William Gunner an attorney.

Even before he became a banker, the local farmers used to leave their money with him, as his iron closet safe was more secure than in their pockets when drinking to celebrate their successful business on the way home.

The countryside around Bishop's Waltham is still famous for its strawberry growing. Conveyancing of the ownership of land used for this crop needed specialist legal knowledge, involving appropriate skills in local solicitors, who in their turn needed specialist help from their bankers. William Gunner, a solicitor as well as a banker, was admirably placed in this respect. Caroline's husband, Charles James, succeeded his father in the law partnership as well as in the bank. Later, when the railway reached Bishop's Waltham, strawberry growing increased, becoming well organized. The strawberries were picked late in the day, loaded on to special trains and at Waterloo unloaded on to carts which took the fruit to Covent Garden early enough in the morning to be sold first thing. This activity proved profitable for the growers, their solicitors and the bank.

The founding partners, though not full-time bankers, took an active part in running the bank. The deed of partnership of 1809 required each partner in turn to attend on two successive days from 12 noon to 3 pm. The aim of the agreement was boldly stated as being '*to increase their respective fortunes.*' To this end a further provision ensured that if any partner lost as much as £100 through a risky investment he should forfeit £2,000 to the other partners. Each partner had originally contributed £1,000 and three of them succeeded in increasing their stake by a modest amount. Stephen Steele, however, proved a liability to the partnership, continuing to overdraw until by 1816 he had accumulated £1,000 of debt. He retired in April that year, having been relegated to the role of sleeping partner for the last twelve months. The remaining three partners then continued until 1834 when Thomas Fox died, at which date the bank became known as Seymour and Gunner, (the names of the remaining partners). During the early part of the century the bank continued to be used by local farmers, the best known of whom was William Cobbett. Considering how angry he had been at the losses sustained by his own farm labourers through the failure of a Salisbury bank it was a considerable compliment to the Bishop's Waltham partners that he should have entrusted them with his own money. The bank was used at this time by a wide variety of customers, from labourers to landowners though some of the latter accounts had to be written off as bad debts. It was observed that the women customers both married and single were most likely to keep their accounts in credit. With the death of John Goulding Seymour in 1840 the bank became a family business known as Gunner & Sons. Mrs Seymour received half the remaining shares and William Gunner took his two sons Charles and Thomas into the partnership. Thomas, however, being less well suited to banking, retired five years later.

Eighteen fifty-one was a year of great change. William Gunner, one of the first partners, retired, moving the short distance to Winchester. John Mansell, clerk to the bank since 1789 when he started on a salary of one guinea a week and was described by William Gunner as *'a man whom I never found in error'* retired with his master. He was succeeded as clerk by his son-in-law, James Lock at £150 a year. Charles James Gunner was now senior partner of Gunner & Co. In addition he was active in the county as Registrar to the County Court, Clerk to the Magistrates and to two Turnpike Trusts, an accumulation of work so heavy that in 1867 he took a partner into his solicitor's office. As partners in the bank in 1851 he took Thomas Fox, of Lambeth, nephew of the original Fox partner, and his own first cousin Thomas John Ridge. Charles James and his wife Caroline, born Hale, had their first child in 1851, followed by another six sons and three daughters. It may be assumed that during this period Caroline had little time to take an interest in the work of the bank. Indeed, her husband was so much engaged with his outside duties that he and his partners met only twice a year, to present accounts, leaving the daily business of the bank to their confidential clerk, James Lock. Though so different from that practised by the original partners, this system of management proved no less effective, with profits continuing an upward trend. There was apparently never any question of amalgamation into a joint stock bank as so many private partnerships were doing.

Another radical change was brought about by the death of Charles in 1872 when Caroline Gunner took over the senior partnership with her cousin Thomas Ridge and Thomas Fox as junior partners. The former died in 1873 and the latter retired five years later, when Caroline, whose children were by then out of the nursery, could give the bank her undivided attention. She had the assistance of James Lock, promoted to managing partner after more than twenty years in the bank. Their success was such that between 1870 and 1890 bank profits doubled from around £1,100 to £2,100. James Lock retired in 1883 and Caroline took her two elder sons, William Henry Ridge Gunner and Charles Richards Gunner into partnership. The former, her elder son, held a commission in the North Lancashire Regiment and continued his army career while his brother remained in Bishop's Waltham and took over the duties of managing partner from James Lock, while their mother kept her place as senior partner until her death in 1906.

During the early years of the twentieth century profits continued healthy especially and somewhat gruesomely just after the 1914-1918 war when the decimated third generation of the Gunner family entered the bank. Walter Robin, the only survivor of Charles Richards Gunner's six sons, joined the partnership in 1918 and his cousin Frank Hugh, the son of William Henry Ridge Gunner, joined in 1923. Ernest John Gunner, one of Caroline's younger sons, perhaps because there were so few of the family left, seemed to feel it his duty to take on the responsibilities of the family bank, joining in 1923 although already in his sixties, and only survived two more years. Caroline's two grandsons continued for longer than any other private bank, until in 1953 the Bishop's Waltham bank business was taken over by Barclays Bank, who appointed as local director one of the surviving partners, Major Frank Hugh Gunner DSO.

Caroline Mary St Barbe. Another Hampshire woman banker, having inherited the bank at Lymington on the death of her husband in 1879, successfully carried on for seventeen years until it merged in 1896 with the Capital and Counties Banking Company. Caroline Mary Stuart Reed was born at Woolwich, where her father Lt Alexander Reid was in the Royal Artillery. She was baptised at St Mary Magdalene 15 August 1817, though in the census of 1851 she gave her age as twenty-seven, suggesting that she was not born until 1824 or 25. She married in 1850 George Foster St Barbe, born 1808, eldest surviving son of Charles St Barbe of Lymington. George, a lieutenant in the Lymington Troop of Yeomanry Cavalry, was previously married to Henrietta Maria Cleveland, who died childless in 1849. Caroline's first child, Charles, was born in 1853, by which date her husband had been a partner in the Lymington bank with his father for many years.

The St Barbe family had long been settled in Lymington, as merchants with interests in salt, coal and sail-making. Charles St Barbe enjoyed a high reputation, honoured in his memorial which states that *'by liberality, uprightness and intelligence in his dealings as a merchant, by impartiality and sound judgment as a magistrate and in his readiness to assist his neighbours both rich and poor, he justly acquired the confidence, esteem and respect of all.'* In 1788 Charles St Barbe senior had opened the family bank in one of a number of houses he owned in Lymington High Street which were used at different dates to suit the bank's varying circumstances. Number 48 was used as bank premises between 1839 and 1844 by Charles St Barbe but by 1871 it had become a school. Numbers 66 to 68 were used by George St Barbe between 1861 and 1878, presumably the year of his death, since by 1881 his widow Caroline was occupying these houses as home and bank. From 1891 to the amalgamation in 1896 number 68 only was used as the bank premises. After merging with Capital and Counties the bank switched its premises once more, now using numbers 66 and 67, presumably leasing number 68 to Caroline for her personal use. A century later, still known as the Old Bank House, the house became first an hotel and more recently, a bistro.

Kent:

SARAH RICE. Sarah Rice came from a sea-faring family. Her father, John Samson (sometimes spelt Sampson) and her uncles Brooke and James were all captains of East India Company ships. The family was of Huguenot stock, settled in East Kent in the seventeenth century, where they manufactured copies of China porcelain, known, and now collected, as Samsonware. Later her own interest in fine china appears in a receipted bill from Josiah Wedgwood. Sarah's mother, Margaret Walton, traced her descent from the Anne Marlowe who kept a public house in Canterbury until 1629, and was the youngest sister of Christopher Marlowe. Sarah was thus his great-great-great niece.

Sarah was born in Whitechapel in 1754 and was brought up by her aunt Rebecca Saure. The latter was the widow Sarah's uncle James Samson, who died when Sarah was only one year old. As a young woman, Sarah was described by a contemporary as *'not exactly handsome, but a smart looking girl.*' She took care of her appearance, sometimes getting her clothes in London; a bill survives for a sarsenet pelisse from R & G Thompson of Cockspur St and another for furs from P Poland & Co, '*next door to the Lyceum, next to the Exeter Change, the Strand.*' The Samson family wealth may not have been without its added attractions. Sarah's dowry was £30,000, or more than half the £50,000 Elizabeth Bennet suggested in *Pride and Prejudice* as a dowry large enough to satisfy '*the younger son of an earl, unless the elder brother were very sickly.*'

A scurrilous story about Sarah's large fortune relates how Captain Henry Rice bet a friend ten guineas that he would succeed in marrying the heiress. If so he was thorough in its execution, bringing his ship, the *Dutton*, into Dover harbour in order to give a ball at which he would propose to Miss Samson. This interesting young man was born in 1743, the son of Walter Rice of Glamorganshire. His uncle David Rice served on and became Commander of the *Dutton*, an East Indiaman. Henry first went to sea age sixteen in 1759/60 on the Warwick, part owned by his uncle. He was appointed third mate in 1764/5. His time at sea, the voyages lasting some fifteen months, took him to Bombay, Madras, the Bay of Bengal and Coromandel, China, Cape Town and St Helena. Henry succeeded in his career, becoming captain of the *Dutton*, and owner of a share in her.

Henry Rice was a lucky man. In 1775 he put in to Cape Town, and found Captain Cook of the *Resolution* on his second voyage of discovery and whose ship was in need of repair. Henry Rice was able to lend him some men to caulk the ship's gaping seams. Also, as he took great interest in new maritime inventions, his Foxon's hydrometer, a current gauge. On reaching St Helena both captains called upon the Governor, M Corneille. Henry also took some important passengers returning from India on his ship '*Mr Graham and his lady, General MacLean and the Honourable Mr Stewart, son of the Earl of Bute.*' Such encounters no doubt proved useful in forwarding his career. An East Indiaman was said to clear £10,000 a voyage so Henry Rice was by no means an ineligible bachelor.

His proposal at the shipboard Ball proved successful and Henry Rice married Sarah Samson on 29 January 1776 when he made generous settlements on his wife and future children. At this date Henry's home was at How Hatch in Essex. His career prospered and he was sworn in first as a younger brother and in 1780 as an Elder Brother of Trinity House. Henry Rice had returned from his last voyage in the *Dutton I*; he had sailed in January 1784 for Madras and Bengal, returning home, after the encounter with Captain Cook in 1775. After this voyage the *Dutton I* was sold, in a coffee house, for £2,000.

Permission was given rather speedily for his building of the *Dutton II*, as the ship was still engaged for another five voyages for the East India Company. In 1780 he was appointed as Commander of the *Dutton II*, which was launched in June 1781. The ship was urgently needed to carry troops to India, so Henry got better terms. Around October of 1881 Henry became a ship's husband, remaining on shore and sharing the profits and losses of the ship. It was noted that Henry Rice did not insure his ship but saw to it that she was copper-bottomed for tropical waters. After this change he ceased to be known as Commander and became Esq. In 1786 the *Dutton* entered Dover Roads again and Henry Rice, as her ship's husband, was welcomed aboard with a salute of eleven guns. After another ten years successful trading, disaster struck in 1796. In a fearful January storm the *Dutton* ran aground in Plymouth harbour. Her captain, Peter Sampson, was ashore but had bravely towed himself through the surf to the ship by a rope. Day by day editions of *The Times* of London described in detail his gallant action and the violence of the storm in which the ship broke up.

Meanwhile Henry Rice bought Bramling (with different spellings) House from the widow of an admiral. It was well suited to a sailor for it commanded a view of the Downs, where so many ships moored while waiting for a favourable wind. The house stood in the parish of Ickham, four miles east of Canterbury, on the Sandwich road. At his death, aged fifty-six, in Bath, in 1797, Henry Rice was described as '*of Bramling House*' and Sarah Rice continued to live here, as well as in Clarence House in Dover. The epitaph '*An honest man is the noblest work of God*' which Sarah inscribed on her husband's tomb in St Mary's church in Dover illustrates her character as much as his.

Henry Rice had other business interests than shipping. An indenture for 23 March 1789 sets out the formation of a bank partnership '*between John Latham and Samuel Latham of the town and port of Dover, merchants, of the first part, Henry Rice Esq of Dover, of the second part, Thomas Larkins of Blackheath Esq of the third part and John Graham of St Lawrence near*

Canterbury of the fourth part.' The indenture states that £5,000 is to be contributed for each of the four parts. These specify £671 annually to the Latham partners and other sums respectively to the other partners. An unusual stipulation was made that partners should not engage in any business but that of the bank, excepting Henry Rice and one other partner, because each was a '*ships husband.*' Sarah presumably took over her husband's bank partnership on his death in 1797 for an indenture of 1811 states that '*the Dover bank of Samuel Latham, Sarah Rice and Henshaw Latham had been in business for these several years last past.*' She retired as second partner that year and her son Edward joined the bank as third partner. By this date the annual sums available to each partner had increased: Samuel Latham £1,600 and Henshaw Latham and Edward Rice £800 each. These were respectable sums in a provincial town but paled into insignificance when compared with the £80,000 drawn by Harriott Coutts from her London bank. (*See Chapter One*)

After her husband's death Sarah Rice, as one of his executors, immediately became active also in her late husband's other concerns. A letter of 14 April 1797 on behalf of Mr Preston of Coutts Bank consults her about continuing the share in a new ship, taken up by her husband with the bank, '*or have the money returned.*' The correspondence does not show whether Mrs Rice availed herself of the generous offer by Coutts to return the money already advanced but she is known to have sold her share in the *Dutton* at this date. Her unusual strength of character was demonstrated in an encounter with the Iron Duke. When a gun-battery was stationed near her house in Dover, she was offended as much by the sight of it as by the sound. She had all the shutters closed and invited the Duke of Wellington, then at Walmer Castle, to call. Mrs Rice explained that she would have to continue in darkness as long as the guns remained, whereupon the Duke gave orders for the battery to be moved forthwith. Such a woman was clearly capable of taking an active part in any business.

Latham, Rice & Co, did not confine their activities to banking, in spite of the restrictions in the 1789 indenture. Describing themselves also as '*merchants and agents,*' they kept a fleet of fast small ships to trade and to obtain news quickly from agents in Calais and other continental ports. For a more speedy return of the information they organized a carrier pigeon service. From this Mrs Rice is believed to have made a great deal of money, personally, through selling to Rothschilds the early news of the defeat of Napoleon at Waterloo. For many years the bank supplied information to the Rothschilds, a connection whose value to the Dover partners is shown later by the somewhat sycophantic nature of a letter of 1815 to the London firm. It apologising for lateness in their receipt of a budget of news, deprecatingly proffers as excuses that the boy and his horse had fallen, the horse's knees badly broken and the boy concussed. It is possible that the letter might have been less humble had Mrs Rice still been a partner.

When her husband died, Sarah's family consisted of two surviving sons (a son and a daughter had died earlier). The elder son Henry, was known to Jane Austen and the Steventon social set. He was up at Christ's College, Cambridge, took Holy Orders, and in 1801 married Lucy, daughter of Isaac and Anne Lefroy, of Ashe, close friends of the Austen family. Henry was described in *Burke's Landed Gentry* on this occasion as being of Sutton Court near Faversham, Kent. Jane Austen described Henry Rice as '*that pleasant boy,*' he being some five years younger than herself. His '*bright eyes*' were perhaps a factor in Jane Austen's accusation of meanness in his mother. Jane Austen wanted Henry to accept the curacy of Deane, the next parish to Steventon and in the gift of her brother James. She was anxious for Mrs Rice to buy Henry the house there and wrote on 14 January 1801 of her hopes that '*Mrs Rice will relent in favour of Deane.*' She was, however doubtful whether Henry could '*persuade a perverse and narrow-minded woman to oblige those whom she does not love.*' On the strength of this description it has been suggested that Jane Austen used Mrs Rice as the model for Fanny Price's disagreeable aunt Norris in *Mansfield Park*. More important, Mrs Rice was also said to have refused Henry his rightful share of his father's estate, and furthermore, persecuted an old relative of her husband with demands for money. There is, however, plenty of evidence to the contrary, showing in fact a most scrupulous fairness in Sarah's financial dealings with her two sons, and that in the second matter, too, she behaved in a fair and even generous manner. First, in respect of Mrs Rice's failure to buy Henry the house at Deane, she had in fact by 1809 bought him the house and living of Great Hollands in Essex. Typically, however, he sold it soon afterwards, to settle a large debt, though continuing to live there as tenant. Henry was reputed to have a passion for gambling and prize-fighting, and in 1813 even his brother-in-law, Christopher Edward Lefroy, had to sue him for a debt. His mother continued to pay his bills, often many years overdue, such as one to a Cambridge tradesman in 1804, long after Henry went down from the university.

Sarah Rice's younger son, Edward Royds Rice, who took over her partnership in the bank in 1811, had been up at Worcester College, Oxford, and married in 1819 Elizabeth, second daughter of Edward Austen Knight of Godmersham in Kent. Edward, who had been adopted by the Knights, was a brother of Jane Austen, adding another literary connection to that with Christopher Marlowe. In 1814 Sarah bought them Danecourt, where they settled and where their fifteen children were born. The house was near Dover, for which Edward was elected Member of Parliament. Mrs Rice's accounts show how equally her money was divided between her two sons. The cost of the living and house at Great Hollands, with the considerable improvements on which Henry embarked, closely resembled the cost of Edward's house, Danecourt. When the sums of money additionally provided for each from their father's estate were included in the calculations, only a few shillings divided the totals, with the tiny balance actually in Henry's favour. It would appear that the character attributed to Mrs Rice, of unfairness to Henry in money matters, based on Jane Austen's letters, is without other foundation. Perhaps '*the pleasant boy*' made the usual impression on a young woman, or Jane Austen may merely have been exercising her not inconsiderable talent for irony. The other matter, the 'persecution' of one of her husband's relations, is also capable of very different interpretation when the evidence is examined.

Family papers show Mrs Rice as a tolerant lender to an unconscionably dilatory debtor. Captain Rice lent money, totalling £1,900 a large sum then, (in 2007 this figure is more than 2-million pounds) in 1791 and 1792, to two relatives, John and his brother, the Revd Richard Rice. On the death of Captain Rice, in 1797, instead of quickly paying back the debt to the widow, the brothers offered an endless series of '*pledges of honour*' and procrastination. One 'pledge' in 1809 was followed by four more in 1810, and a letter promising regular payments to clear the interest was sent in 1814. In 1817 Mrs Rice's solicitor received a letter from a Mr Ward, promising an immediate large payment from Richard

Rice. Mr Ward offered his Irish estates as security *'but so as not to make himself personally liable.'* Mrs Rice thereupon instructed her solicitor (her buyer's bill was then two pounds 6 shillings and 8 pence) to make regular enquiries at her London bankers, Barnett Hoares, whether this large sum had been paid. In May and August 1817, and in February and April of 1818, he was told that *'it had not'* though Mrs Rice's bill had mounted to five pounds 13 shillings and 4 pence. In spite of the procrastination Mrs Rice did not take punitive measures. A letter from her lawyer notes that she is *'desired that I would write to Mr Ward previous to my commencing proceedings,'* a generous warning in the circumstances.

Sarah Rice, together with the other two executors, Sir Henry Oxenden, Bart, and Samuel Latham Esq, was responsible for dividing her husband's estate between her sons, and it is clear that she was personally involved in a great deal of trouble and expense in collecting the money due to the estate. The accounts of the loan show great attention to detail, the tax paid on the mortgaged property being deducted from the sum owing as scrupulously as the interest was added to it; for example the interest from 5 July 1811 to 25 May 1813, calculated as £132. 3 shillings and 4 pence had property tax of £13. 4 shillings and 4 pence deducted, *'leaving £118. 19 shillings.'* In the event, the debt was not cleared until 28 June 1830, nearly forty years from the date when the loan was made.

The records indicate that Mrs Rice was as meticulous in money matters concerning her husband's relatives as in those of his estate. The discrepancy in the stories of Mrs Rice and the reality may be due perhaps to a less equal distribution of affection. Her grandchildren kept very different memories of her. These included such disagreeable memories as in general *'a horrible old woman,'* for more particularly that *'she would not let me put my elbows on the arms of my little chair.'* One recalled her merely as *'eccentric, wearing a bonnet, a large white silk one, in house and out,'* and one even remembered her as *'good-natured and kind.'* It could be that Grandmamma Rice was fonder of some than of others of her grandchildren, and perhaps the same might be true of her sons. There is a pathetic post-script to a letter from Henry, when a boy, thanking his mother for the £5 note *'which you was so good as to send me,'* asking *'pray send me a reply, if only a line.'* The phrase has an odd echo years later in a letter from Henry to his mother's solicitor. At the end of one of a series of letters asking for money for the improvements to Great Hollands Henry added '*pray send me a line by return of post.*' Henry would seem to have been always short of money, and always begging, but for a friendly response as much as for the cash. Henry complained to his Steventon friends of his mother's unfairness in money, but his real resentment was identified by Jane Austen in the phrase about Mrs Rice not obliging one '*whom she does not love.*'

The absence from the papers, so carefully kept by Sarah Rice, of any begging letters from Edward, his very prudent marriage into the local landed gentry, his election to Parliament and his partnership in the bank, all suggest a radically different character from that of his older brother. It is not difficult to see which would appeal more strongly to their business-like mother. Nevertheless, no matter how unequally her affection may have been distributed, in her financial arrangements she was painstakingly honest, and not ungenerous in business dealings.

Sarah Rice died in Dover in 1842 aged eighty-seven. By this time she had become something of an institution and it was said that letters addressed only to Mrs Rice, Dover, reached her. Her funeral was a grand affair. Five mourning coaches, the newspaper stated, drove through the town to St Mary's church and her obituary describes her as '*the much respected mother of our excellent representative.*' With her usual thoroughness Sarah wrote a will of twenty-one pages. She remembered her charitable interests, leaving money to buy coals for the widows of the seamen of Dover '*to be distributed on Christmas Eve by the mayor or other authority.*' Her marriage settlement stated that after the death of Henry and Sarah three trustees were to administer an undefined amount of annuities to the surviving children. The four executors of her will were these three trustees and her second son Edward Royds Rice. The interest on £13,000 was to go to Henry, to be administered by trustees for his lifetime and after his death the interest on £3,000 to his wife Lucy. The interest on the remaining £10,000 to his surviving daughter, goddaughter of Sarah, Sarah Hodgson wife of Douglas Hodgson. The money was to be paid to Sarah and '*not for the debts of her husband or any other husband she may happen to marry*' and then to their children. Edward Royds Rice inherited all Sarah's carriages, horses, furniture and household goods. He also received her landed estates, in trust for his eldest surviving son. The trustees were instructed to set aside

£20,000 from her leasehold and personal estate for the other children, to be shared equally and paid to them when they were twenty-one. Various diamonds were left to Lizzy as long as she remained Edward's widow.

Sarah Rice had clearly given thorough consideration to the way in which she could leave her large fortune to give most benefit to her two very different surviving sons. Henry was to be supported, her female relations were to be trusted, and the important part of her estate, the land, was to go to Edward and then to his male descendants. Sarah Rice undoubtedly possessed the carefulness and strength of character essential for a successful business woman.

ELEANOR MARY DOORNE, Executor/partner. The notice of dissolution of partnership in the London Gazette of 1811 was signed by Eleanor Mary Doorne as Widow and Administratrix for her late husband Stephen Doorne at Rochester in Kent. The bank was founded as Day & Day in 1782 and Stephen, described in the poll book of 1807 as gentleman, is listed as a bank partner in 1806. He was dead by 1811, although his name appears in later lists. At this date Eleanor Mary Doorne describing herself as widow and administratrix signed '*for Self and executrix*' thus indicating that she was taking part in the bank on her own account as well as in the position of executor. This bank continued until taken over by the Provincial Banking Corporation in 1864.

Surrey:

ELIZABETH LA COSTE. The La Costes were multiple traders, owners of the Abbey Mill, successor to the mills of Chertsey Abbey, and at different dates described themselves as mealmen, corn dealers and millers. Thomas La Coste enlarged the family interests by opening a bank first recorded in 1808, by which date he was already married to Elizabeth, with a three-year-old son, Thomas Blake, later to follow him in the bank. Elizabeth herself took an interest in social problems, and in 1810 was involved with the Female Friendly Society, being listed as an Honorary Member in the Rule Book of that date.

By 1812 two more partners, William Clarke and Durley Grazebrook, had joined the bank and the partnership renewed their licence to issue their own notes at both Chertsey and Egham. Their issue, a modest sum suitable for a small bank, amounted to £3,400 in 1846. This was an eventful year for the bank, Thomas having recently died and Elizabeth taken his place as senior partner, with their son Thomas Blake La Coste. Elizabeth carried on the bank successfully until she died, before 1851, leaving her son in charge. The bank continued as La Coste & Co. The business was bought in 1876 by a neighbouring private bank, Thomas Ashby of Staines. The Ashby family were corn dealers and mealmen like the La Costes and the two banks of the latter, at Chertsey and Egham, were continued as branches by the Ashbys until they in their turn were merged in 1888 with Barclays Bank.

Sussex:

LEONORA TILDEN SAMPSON. This banker differed both from the La Coste traders and the military bankers at Reading. She was born into a Sussex landed family, the daughter of James and Mary Markwick of Catsfield, where she was baptised on 20 August 1741. Leonora's mother's family, the Eversfields, were headed by Charles Eversfield who inherited the baronetcy of Fermor but died without an heir in 1784. His sister Olive died aged ninety in 1803 leaving her fortune to her nephew William Markwick, Leonora's brother, who accordingly took the name and arms of Eversfield for himself and his issue. William had two sons, Charles and James, the younger of whom sold Catsfield and moved to Denne Place, Horsham, where in 1822 he was High Sheriff of Sussex. James died in 1825 leaving a two-year-old son, Charles Gilbert, who died without issue in 1886 when once again the name of Eversfield became extinct in the direct line. Leonora's husband came from another well established Sussex family; in August 1783 she married John Tilden of Battle, who had been baptised there on 4th December 1741. Coincidentally, he too was left a family name, inheriting from his kinsman Richard Sampson Gent of Ninfield, Sussex, his estate and name. Richard was buried at Ninfield in June 1779. The change of name, however, was not registered until November 1797.

The Sampsons had lived in Sussex since the middle of the seventeenth century. Richard Sampson's great-grandfather started as a distiller; he was a Freeman of Pevensey in 1683 and of Ninfield from 1696. He died in 1715 leaving distillers' shops at both these places together with farms and lands at Bexhill, Hurstmonceux and

Crowhurst. Two more generations of Richard Sampsons succeeded in possession of these estates before they came to John Tilden. The bank first appeared at Hastings in 1791 as Tilden, Smith, Hilder and Gill, quoted in the Bankers' magazine of 1845 as '*Tilden, Smith, Hilde and Gill, all four for a one-pound bill.*' This couplet contains the only mention to Smith at this date, another reference being Tilden Shadwell, Hilder, Harvey and Gill. Shadwell disappears from the partnership after 1793, after which there was no change for some years. In 1810 the firm is listed as Tilden Sampson & Co. John Tilden Sampson died that year although he still appears as senior partner in one of the two entries for the Hastings bank in the 1813 Leekey's list of banks issuing their own notes. The other entry was headed by Leonora Tilden Sampson, without her husband. In both entries the other partners were John Hilder, William Harvey and William Gill. Leonora had in fact been senior partner for the last three years since her husband's death and although nearly seventy, having no succeeding generations to look to, she was able to devote her time to profitable banking. The bank not only operated at Hastings but had opened branches at Battle, Robertsbridge, Eastbourne and Bexhill.

Clearly this bank exerted a major influence in Sussex business life. The strength of the bank may have been due in some measure to the long-standing friendships between the partners. In Ninfield Leonora carried on the lease of some woodland in 1815 with William Harvey, land which he had originally leased with her husband in 1796. Another of the original partners, William Lucas Shadwell, a surgeon at Hastings, appears more than twenty years later as the principal Trustee of Leonora's will. The Smith family, who dropped out of the partnership in the 1790s, must have kept in touch for Leonora welcomed them back into the bank in 1816, the year she retired. She died two years later and by 1830 the senior partner was Tilden Smith, with two younger members of his family, Tilden Smith junior and Francis Smith. The two latter were still partners when the bank failed in 1857. Disaster came '*in consequence of clamours from the creditor*' and according to the article in the Bankers' magazine was wrongly attributed to the two Smith brothers. Nevertheless their property had to be sold at auction and raised £16,000. The property for sale consisted of the Vine Hall estate with mansion, farm, 36 cottages, public house and 578 acres.

The bank had made large profits over many years and Leonora died a rich woman. At her death in 1818 she disposed meticulously of the property, leaving Tilden portraits, for instance, to members of her husband's family. Similarly, portraits of Markwicks and Eversfields, from her side of the family, were bequeathed to her sister-in-law Mrs Eversfield. To her niece Sophia Eversfield Leonora left her pearl necklace and her diamond earrings and pin, leaving the rest of her jewellery to her Tilden nieces. Their brother John received, as well as personal bequests, a large part of her landed property. On the other hand their father, her husband's brother George, was summarily dismissed with a bequest of £100 whereas his wife Mary was left the interest on the considerable remainder of Leonora's estate. The bequest stated that Mary was to receive the legacy '*for her sole and disparate use being independent of any debts contracts or engagements of her present husband or any future husband.*' Leonora states that her sister-in-law shall have the money whether '*sole or couverte,*' the legal term for single or married. This clause is another reminder that at this date a married woman could not own property unless through a trust Leonora thus indicates that from her own experience she had faith in a woman's ability to make the best use of her own property.

Chapter Six

Widows inheriting banks from their husbands

East Anglia: **SARAH CRICKITT**, *Colchester, Chelmsford, Ipswich, Swaffham.*
Essex: **CHARLOTTE COX**, *Harwich*; **MARGARET ROUND**, *Colchester.*
Suffolk: **GRACE MARRATT**, *Hadleigh Manningtree*; **REBECCA ALEXANDER**, *Ipswich*; **ANNA SOPHIA ALEXANDER**, *Ipswich.*
Lincolnshire: **CHARLOTTE ANN EATON**, *Stamford*; **SUSAN CLAYPON**, *Boston.*
Norfolk: **FRANCES ELIZABETH HARVEY**, *Norwich.*

East Anglia:
SARAH CRICKITT. The family of Sarah Dolby, born in 1744, were possessed of a considerable fortune, through carrying on a lucrative trade with Portugal. In 1768 they bought a hundred year lease of a mansion, Brises, at Kelvedon Hatch near Brentwood. This house was described as '*a good old house*,' built by Thomas Bryce circa 1498, though other sources date it from 1720. However that may be, the house was extensively re-built as '*a splendid brick box with nine bay windows.*' Sarah must have been brought up to understand the importance of having a good head for business. This would undoubtedly have been a help to her husband. She married, at the age of twenty-three, Charles Alexander Crickitt of Smyths Hall, Blackmore, Essex, also known as Copsheaves or Ruddocks. He opened the bank of Crickitt & Co at Colchester in 1774 soon after their marriage. Having completed the building of the bank in 1776 he expanded his influence by opening banks at Ipswich and Chelmsford, and a branch at Maldon.

The Crickitt family were Huguenots who had been settled since the late seventeenth century in Colchester and the Dutch church there contains monuments to the family, including one to Sarah's son Robert Alexander Crickitt. This church, however, is one of the places where the alternative spelling, Crickett, is found, though the most convincing evidence is for the form used here. Charles was active in many ways, as Recorder in 1787, High Steward of Colchester in 1788, Receiver General in 1795 and MP for Ipswich from 1784 until his death in 1803. He was so devoted to the Tory party that the bank was known as the Blue Bank, in opposition to Gurney, Alexander & Co of the Yellow Bank, keen supporters of the Liberal interest Charles Crickitt's enthusiasm for the Tory cause led to his being involved in a duel with a radical Whig, the Revd Nicholas Corsellis of Wivenhoe, in 1789. Fortunately for Charles, the latter, perhaps in deference to his cloth, fired into the air, '*a harmless ending*,' according to the local newspaper. Sarah and Charles had a large family, two sons, Charles Alexander and Robert Alexander, and six daughters.

At her husband's death in 1803 Sarah, now aged fifty-nine, took on his partnership in all three banks. As senior partner Sarah proved so efficient that for 20 years the Colchester bank was considered '*one of the best managed banks in the kingdom.*' Unfortunately her sons did not inherit their mother's managerial skills. Her elder son, Charles junior, retired in 1789 after a very short time in the partnership. Her second son Robert followed his father as MP for Ipswich, from 1807 to 1825 but his election expenses ruined the bank. He drew on Chelmsford and Maldon banks to the tune of £16,500, on Colchester for £28,000 and on Ipswich for £13,000, resulting in the failure of Crickitt & Co at Chelmsford in the crisis of 1825–26. The bank stopped payment on 24 December 1825, the partners then being Sarah Crickitt, Robert Alexander Crickitt and Samuel Hunt Russell. As a result of the failure, the Chelmsford partners were declared bankrupt, but the banks at Colchester and Ipswich were able to continue under partners who had not been involved. Advertisements appeared in the local press on 17 March 1826 of the sale by auction of the household effects of Mrs Crickitt of Smyths Hall, Blackmore, and on 4 April of those of her son Robert in Colchester.

The surviving business of the Chelmsford bank was taken over by another East Anglian bank, Sparrow and Co. Smyth Hall, in which Sarah had lived since her marriage and which had been the family home for her children until their marriages, was now sold. Nevertheless, perhaps with the help of her brother Charles Jeremiah Dolby, Sarah was able to move into Priors, a manor not far from her brother who was still living in the Dolby estate of Brises at Kelvedon Hatch. The effects of a bankruptcy such as that of Crickitt were noted and felt, well beyond the immediate neighbourhood. On February 15th 1826 the Provost of Oriel College, Oxford, Mr E Cobblestone, wrote to his agent C C Parker, asking whether Crickitt's bank were likely to pay a large dividend, adding that *'from rumours that have reached me, I fear the reverse. It would, however, be some satisfaction to know which of my own farmers, and to what extent they are involved in this failure.'*

Essex:

CHARLOTTE COX. Charlotte Cox is listed in 1845 in the partnership of Bridges & Co at Harwich. Her husband, Anthony Cox, senior, born in 1767, was a partner in this bank at Harwich, Hadleigh and Manningtree from 1810, and before that had, for some years, been the government agent for the packet boats to Holland. Later he became Mayor of Harwich and Deputy Lieutenant for Suffolk. Their son Anthony, born in 1810, joined the bank as partner by 1835 and like his father was Mayor of Harwich. Anthony Cox senior died in 1839 aged seventy-two but his son was only thirty-two when he died soon after in 1842. Charlotte Cox, thus doubly bereft, inherited the senior partnership in the Harwich bank. In 1845 her partners there were William Rodwell, John Cobbold and his son John Chevalier Cobbold, who were also all Ipswich solicitors and partners in the Ipswich bank of Crickitt & Co from which Sarah Crickitt had been forced to retire in 1826 after the bankruptcy at Chelmsford. The Cobbold family had been brought into the Ipswich bank in 1829 as their flourishing business as brewers, maltsters and corn traders was expected to be an asset to the partnership. Charlotte Cox's bank in Harwich amalgamated in 1893, many years after her death, with Bacon and Cobbold, bankers at Ipswich. This bank merged with Capital & Counties in 1899, absorbed in its turn by Lloyds in 1900.

MARGARET ROUND. The part played by the vagaries of fate are only too well demonstrated by comparing the destiny of Sarah Crickitt with that of Margaret Round, another woman partner in the surviving Crickitt Colchester bank. Margaret, daughter of General Borthwick, married on 5 October 1824 George, son of George Round senior of Lexden House in the parish of St Peter's, Colchester, who had died in August 1823. The senior branch of the family lived in Birch Hall in Essex, bought by James Round, 'citizen of London' in 1724. James having died without leaving a son was succeeded there by his brother William, George's father. George's mother died after eight years of marriage in 1809 so that George junior, their second child, must have been born around 1803 or 1804. George Round senior joined the established bank of Crickitt & Co at Colchester in 1790, remaining in the partnership until his death in 1823. His son George junior was a partner in the bank from this date until he died in 1857, leaving his share in the bank to his wife Margaret. When the Chelmsford bank of Crickitt & Co broke in the crisis of 1825 (cf *p. 146*) the Colchester bank of Crickitt, Round & Co saved themselves through the support of their customers, 400 of whom signed a bill dated 17 December 1825. '*We the undersigned being satisfied of the solvency of the Colchester bank of the firm Crickitt, Round, Pattison & Co which has no connection with any other banking establishment do hereby pledge ourselves to take the notes of the above firm and to give it every support in our possession.*' This testimony may have originated from the championship of the Revd William Marsh DD, the rector of St Peter's, Colchester, in whose parish the Round family lived.

> '*On one occasion, during a commercial crisis in the country, a panic occurred on market day in Colchester which seemed likely to prove ruinous to a highly respectable banking house in the town. The farmers and many other depositors who had assembled for the market rushed to draw out their money and the run on the bank was great. Dr Marsh, having in his house a considerable sum of money in cash, at once put it in a bag, took it across to the bank, and paid it into his account, in spite of the assurances of the bystanders that the bank was just about to break. Taking heart, one by one they went away. Dr Marsh remained until the closing hour, confidence was restored, and the bank was saved.*'

This intrepid clergyman was more sensible to the imminent danger to the Colchester bank because he had been giving shelter to his mother Catherine at his vicarage. Ten years previously her extravagance had been largely responsible for the failure of their family bank at Reading.

After the Crickitt members of the bank had retired it was reorganized, becoming Round, Green, Green and Pattison in 1826. In that year the Egerton Green family began their long association with this bank and Joshua Pattison who had for many years been a clerk, joined the partnership in which he continued until his death in 1845. In 1826 the bank was still drawing on the same London agent, Sir James Esdaile & Co, who must also have felt confidence in the new partnership. Esdailes themselves failed some years later, in 1837. At this time Joseph Hoare, the London banker, realised that the failure of the agent would affect the Colchester bank and came to their rescue. He was not wholly disinterested in Colchester, having married a daughter of the Buxton family, partners in several East Anglian banks. He at once left London bringing a large quantity of money. Unluckily he was asked to pay a pound in advance for the chaise and found he had no small change with him. Not daring to open his bag he had to leave his watch in pawn. On arrival at Colchester he was met by an anxious Egerton Green who asked him to take over the agency. By this means the Colchester partners were able to continue, another illustration of a bank's survival through a combination of enterprise and good luck such as was shown by the intervention of Dr Marsh in Colchester. It is to be hoped that Mr Hoare successfully reclaimed his watch.

In 1857 when Margaret Round took over her late husband's share in the bank, her partners were John and Henry Egerton Green who had joined the year before. Margaret, as senior partner brought in first of all, in 1861 Horace George Egerton Green and later in 1866 Edward Augustus Round, presumably her son, who predeceased her in 1876. During Margaret's leadership of the bank, business prospered. A branch was opened at Brightlingsea, a town which developed into a considerable centre for sailing and fisheries including oyster beds for the Colchester natives. A new building for the bank was opened in 1879 and business was strengthened in 1883 by Margaret inviting Charles Richard Gurney Hoare to join the partnership, thus reinforcing a connection with Barnett Hoare's London bank and with the Gurneys of Earlham, bankers in many East Anglian towns. Margaret died in 1886, leaving a successful bank to merge eventually with Gurneys in 1891 to form Gurney, Round, Green and Hoare, her name being kept for the goodwill. Later they acquired Mills & Bawtree, another large local bank and amalgamated with Barclays in 1896 when the surviving partners became the local directors.

In contrast with Margaret Round's Colchester bank's amalgamation with Barclays, Charlotte Cox's bank in Ipswich ended with Lloyds. Through their choice of partners the two survivors of the Crickitt group became constituent members of two different banks in the then existing 'Big Five.'

Suffolk:

GRACE MARRATT. The name Marratt appears, confusingly, at different dates in two East Anglian partnerships, in three towns. At Hadleigh and at Harwich, in 1810 the bank was Bridges & Marratt. In 1812 the bankers there were John, Richard & John Jnr. Mills, Thomas, Nunn & John Brownrigge Leake & Grace Marratt. Her name appears in the same partnership at this date in Manningtree. The IG Index records a marriage between a Grace Phillebrown and John Marriatt (*sic*) on 31 March 1791 at Mistley. If this entry can be identified with Grace and John Marratt the 1810 partnerships of Marratt with Bridges would be explained by the fact that this bank operated at Mistley as well as at Manningtree. John Marratt presumably died before 1812 as only Grace Marratt's name is listed, at that date at Hadleigh and Manningtree. She then appears in the rival partnership of Mills, Nunn & Co. An explanation for her change of allegiance may perhaps be found in the topographical distribution of the other partners in both banks. Grace Marratt may well have preferred to join a partnership with Hadleigh neighbours.

Thomas Nunn lived at Lawford House in Hadleigh and John Brownrigg Leake was a busy lawyer there, much involved with the life of the parish. He gave a gilt alms dish to the church in 1793 and in 1806 his name as churchwarden was inscribed on the fifth bell. On the other hand, among the partners in Bridges & Co, the bank from which the name Marratt disappeared, Peter Godfrey lived at East Bergholt and was a Harwich banker, as was Anthony Cox. Grace Marratt retired from the banks at Hadleigh and Manningtree in 1815. At Hadleigh the bank continued

84

until its last listing in 1827. At Manningtree the Nunn family partnership remained in business until 1870 when they merged with the London and County Bank & Co, absorbed in turn by the Westminster Bank.

REBECCA ALEXANDER. The marriage between Rebecca Biddle and Samuel Alexander in 1805 connected several East Anglian Quaker banking families. Through the Lloyds of Dolobran, the Birmingham Quaker bankers, the Cobbold and Cox families, the Alexanders and the Buddles were all connected. Elizabeth, daughter of Sampson Lloyd of Bordesley, married '*John Biddle Esq late of Neach Hill, Shropshire, now of Leamington*' and her younger sister Agatha married Joseph Biddle of Birmingham. The Alexander connection began with the marriage of Dykes Alexander, a banker in Ipswich into the Biddle family and it was his grandson Samuel, who was Rebecca's husband. Samuel's mother was Elizabeth, daughter of John Gurney who opened the Norwich bank in 1775, further illustration of the prevailing influence of Quakers in East Anglian banking.

The Alexanders had been Quakers since William, son of the rector of Otley in Suffolk (who died in 1681) was imprisoned for his faith. Samuel and Rebecca's first child was born in 1806 and, the family increasing rapidly, in 1809 they bought land just outside Ipswich on which they built Goldrood, a house large enough to hold them and all twelve of their children.

Goldrood House in Suffolk

The plain style of living expected of Quakers was not enforced at its firmest here. Painting would not have been encouraged by strict Quakers but fortunately for us, one of Rebecca's younger daughters, Mary Ann, was allowed to paint elegant little water-colours of interiors and garden scenes. Her charming pictures show a more lavish way of life in Goldrood than would have been appropriate in a conventional Quaker household of the period, though they had no more than six servants, fewer than might be expected in a house of that size. As well as the various rooms Mary Ann drew members of the family elegantly dressed and servants carrying out their daily tasks. She painted the servant's hall with the table laid for Christmas dinner, complete with sprigs of holly, a festival not usually celebrated so traditionally by the Friends. The Alexanders had a wonderful view of the river, for which, no doubt, the site was chosen, with large gardens, also lovingly illustrated by Mary Ann.

When in 1838 Rebecca Alexander took over from her late husband his partnership in Alexander and Cornwell, the Ipswich bank, it had for more than fifty years been known as the Yellow Bank. Its support for the Whig cause had during all this time famously been in conflict with the Tory Blue bank of Crickitt & Co, their rivals in Ipswich banking. Rebecca and Samuel's numerous family provided a source of strong continuity in the bank. When Rebecca took over the partnership her son John Biddle Alexander also joined what was already a family concern. Her husband's uncle, Dykes Alexander the younger, had been in the firm since 1795, his sons Richard and Henry joining him in 1812. Not only were the family successful bankers but over many years were generous benefactors to the town, for instance to education for girls. Henry Alexander founded the Girl's Free School of Industry and carried it on entirely at his own expense. He lived in the town, next door to the bank in a quiet road near St Mary Key, still known as Bank Street. His enthusiasm for similar good causes was one expression of his energetic support for the Whig cause. Rebecca's son-in-law, who was also her husband's first cousin, William Henry, formed part of the intellectual side of the family, reorganizing the public library and supporting the Mechanics' Institution. He joined the bank with Rebecca in 1838, remaining a partner during her lifetime and afterwards until his own death in 1864.

Rebecca's third and fourth sons, George and Frederick, joined the Ipswich partnership when she retired in 1845, though the latter, living in Woodbridge, concerned himself mainly with the branch there which had been opened in 1804. From her retirement until her death in 1849 Rebecca continued to live in her handsome house, Goldrood.

Anna Alexander, Rebecca's daughter-in-law

ANNA SOPHIA ALEXANDER. After Rebecca's son John Biddle Alexander died in 1863, his widow, Anna Sophia, profiting by her mother-in-law's example, became a partner at the age of fifty-three. She was the daughter of John and Ann Phillips of Vauxhall in Surrey, and was married at Wandsworth on 2 June 1836. She joined Frederick Alexander, who had been in the partnership since Rebecca retired in 1845. The bank remained a family business, for another new partner, Samuel Alexander Maw, was related to both the Alexanders and the Gurneys. With them were Anna Sophia's son Samuel and her two nephews Joseph and William. She continued active for more than fifteen years in an unchanged partnership until a new one was formed with their fellow Quakers, the Gurneys, in 1878. Anna Sophia died in 1883 at the age of seventy-three.

In the new firm the Alexanders were represented by Frederick, now aged sixty-four, Anna Sophia's son Samuel and her nephew William. Frederick retired from the new partnership in 1882 and died the following year, described in his obituary as possessing the typical Quaker virtues, so essential to a banker, of being scrupulously just and conscientious. The Alexander Bank continued as a private partnership until their amalgamation with Barclays Bank in 1896. The Alexander family had enjoyed a remarkably long period in business since Samuel Alexander I opened a bank and began trading as a ship owner and dealer in corn and iron at Needham Market in 1744.

Lincolnshire:

CHARLOTTE ANN EATON. The story of this banker begins with another Quaker, her maternal grandfather, Jonathan Ormston, who was born in Kelso in 1708. Wishing to succeed in business as did many Quakers he left home in his twenties for London. After some years of hard work, he returned to Northumberland having earned enough to join with others in founding a bank in 1787 in Newcastle. His daughter Ann married her cousin George Waldie of Hendersyde Park in Roxburghshire. Charlotte Ann was their daughter. Although a Scottish family, the Waldies also had a seat, Kingswood, in Northumberland, where no doubt the cousins, the Ormston and Waldie often met in the Newcastle social round. The Waldies must also have spent some of their time travelling in Europe, for Charlotte, a successful authoress before her marriage, made use of these journeys. Her first book entitled *Narrative of a Residence in Belgium during the Campaign of 1815, and a visit to the Field of Waterloo* ran through many editions. Her second, equally successful book, *Rome in the Nineteenth Century* was illustrated by steel plate engravings and plans. In

1822 Charlotte married Stephen Eaton, who had inherited Dene Park near Thrapstone (or Thrapston) in Northamptonshire, to which he brought his wife and where they raised their family, two sons and two daughters. The Stamford bank which Stephen Eaton joined in 1810 was a well-established business, having been founded in 1800 as Jackson & Co. As senior partner Stephen had been known for his quick temper, once striking a clergyman whom he thought to have cast doubts on his honesty. The customer had jokingly suggested that a pile supposedly of fifty pound notes had been made to look larger by including notes of only one pound, a witticism not taken in good part.

When her husband died in 1834 their elder son Charles Ormston Eaton was only seven years old, and Charlotte took over the senior partnership of the bank. She promoted Robert Michelson, who for many years had been a clerk in the bank, to partnership, though continuing to make important business decisions herself. Charlotte was strong minded though better controlled than her late husband. Characteristically, when the Uppingham branch was in danger from a run, she quelled the crowd of depositors by the force of her personality, speaking to them so firmly that they decided to go home, no longer demanding to withdraw their money and so saved her bank. An historian of early Lincolnshire banks, noted with surprise that there was a woman partner at Stamford. Commenting on her energetic role in the partnership he went so far as to mention that Mrs Eaton *'was by no means a sleeping partner.'*

On her death in 1859 Charlotte's position as senior partner passed to her elder son, Charles Ormston Eaton of Tolethorpe Hall in Rutland. He carried on the Stamford Private Bank until it amalgamated in 1891 with the Stamford, Spalding and Boston joint stock banking company in which he became a director and in which his son Hubert, Charlotte's grandson, became managing director three years later. This local joint stock bank was acquired by Barclays in 1911, one-hundred-and-one years after the Eatons began their connection with the Stamford bank. During this period the family, already considerable landowners, were able to add to their estates by acquiring houses such as Tolethorpe Hall. The longevity of this family bank provide, however, not only prosperity for the partners, but also security and success for their town.

SUSAN or SUSANNA CLAYPON. Susan Bury was born in Winchester in Hampshire in 1794, the daughter of William Fleetwood Bury, a man with property in Wales at Pan-y-Goitre, County Monmouth. Susanna married Joseph Claypon, a banker in Boston, Lincolnshire, but by 1852 they were living in Hyde Park Gardens in Totteridge, Middlesex. Joseph died there in 1859, leaving Susan his residual legatee, though the bank in Boston is not specifically mentioned in his will.

Susan took over as a partner in Garfit and Claypon, joining a well-established concern, begun by a relative of her husband in the first town in Lincolnshire to begin banking. William Garfit, born in 1700, was well into his middle age when he opened his doors for business in 1754 in Boston. Not surprisingly, after twenty years he brought in a partner, his great-nephew, Bartholomew Claypon, Susan's father-in-law. The families intermarried, Bartholomew's daughter marrying a Garfit. When William Garfit the founder died in 1783 Bartholomew Claypon became senior partner, the bank style being Claypon, Garfit & Co though by 1813 the senior partner was William Garfit II, with Bartholomew Claypon and William Garfit III. By 1826 the next generation, the brothers Joseph and Bartholomew Claypon II had joined the bank and later in that decade the bank is listed as Claypon, Garfit and Claypons, with Bartholomew Claypon I, William Garfit III, Joseph Claypon and Bartholomew Claypon II. William Garfit III died in his eighty-third year in July 1856 and the consequent changes among the two families meant that two years later Joseph Claypon had become senior partner, with Bartholomew Claypon II, William Garfit IV and Thomas Garfit.

This was therefore a long-established family bank when in 1859 Joseph Claypon died and Susan entered the partnership. She, like Mrs Eaton at Stamford, took her confidential clerk, John Ingoldby, into the partnership. Through him she was able, even when living at a distance, to bring her influence to bear on the running of the bank. Several innovations soon followed, first the property was enlarged in 1863 by the purchase of the shop next door which was then pulled down and rebuilt to house the bank. In 1865 the partners made an unprecedented New Year present of £1,000 to be divided between agents and clerks, a gift which no doubt provided a considerable incentive. The Claypon bank survived the economic depression which had a disastrous effect on Gee & Co, the other Boston bank. The Stamford Mercury of 4 December 1874 described a run started by 'a *malicious rumour*' at Spilsby. The bank's solid foundation was shown by the fact that many local worthies were prepared to vouch for its solvency so that although on the Saturday several people came to withdraw their deposits, by Monday they returned to pay their money in again. '*That it was so soon stopped is unquestionably due to the promptitude and vigour with which applications were met, to say nothing of the cordiality and goodwill with which they were treated, and many left the bank regretting that they had ever entered it for such a purpose as throwing suspicion on persons they had known so long.*' Indeed, some customers had asked for their deposits in Claypon notes rather than in those of the Bank of England, at which they looked askance; some clients at that date could be somewhat naive about banking, though a local shopkeeper did well by buying in Claypon's notes at a discount and making a profit when the bank successfully withstood the run.

John Ingoldby, with his wife and seven children and two servants, were living in Market Square, where he could keep a close eye on the premises. Later, as a widower, he moved into Paradise Row, an elegant terrace house, at the back of the bank, facing the church. He died aged eighty-nine in 1884, having continued active enough to be described in the census of 1881 as a banker. That year Susan Claypon died, having appointed John Ingoldby as one of her executors, together with William Ward Claypon Lane Claypon (*sic*). Since Joseph and Susan had no children he had appointed his great nephew to be their heir. William W C L Claypon was the son of Joseph's niece Jane and the Revd Charlton Lane. He took additionally the name of Claypon in 1877, when he came to Lincolnshire, building Tytton Hall in Wyberton, and entering the bank partnership. At Susan's death he inherited her Lincolnshire estates and her silver and plate. She also made a generous bequest of £10,000 to his father. Her personal estate amounted to £28,413, showing how well she had prospered as a banker. Her bank continued to flourish after her death in 1881, her great-nephew continuing in the partnership in 1888 with William Garfit V, Thomas Cheney Garfit and Bartholomew Claypon Garfit.

Throughout the century the Boston bank became the centre of a widespread network operating ten branches and agencies at different dates, the earliest from 1800, from Grimsby in the north of the county through Skegness to their southern boundary at Spalding and Bourne. In 1891 the bank merged with Capital and Counties Banking Company which was absorbed by Lloyds.

Norfolk:

FRANCES ELIZABETH HARVEY, executor/partner. In Norwich Frances Elizabeth Harvey is listed as executrix in 1812 for Francis Falton, partner in the Norwich and Swaffham bank of Day, Dalton and Day, established in 1795. It can be presumed that she was one of the several daughters christened Frances Elizabeth in the Dalton families, who married a Harvey. In 1825, more than ten years later, the partnership was bankrupt, under three members of the Day family.

Chapter Seven

Widows inheriting banks from their husbands: Cheshire and Yorkshire

Cheshire: **ELIZABETH PATTON**, *Chester.*
Yorkshire: **MARY RICHARDSON**, *Whitby*; **MARY RIMINGTON**, *Sheffield.*

Cheshire:

ELIZABETH PATTON. The daughter of Obadiah and Anne Denman, Elizabeth was baptised on the 2nd March 1737. The Denman family came from Derbyshire to join in the lead mining boom around Halkyn, in Flintshire, and had been successful enough for their listing in directories to advance from that of 'yeomen' to that of 'gentry.'

Elizabeth was twice married, firstly to John Jones, bachelor of Mold, on 9 August 1772, at Halkyn Parish Church by special licence, considered to be socially correct by aspiring gentry. They had one child, a daughter, baptised Anne Wynne on 19 March 1774. Elizabeth remained so attached to her first husband John that she left instructions to be buried with him in the vault of their parish church at Mold. She was married again now in her late forties, in November 1785 to Thomas Patton Esq, also by special licence, in the Parish Church of St Oswalds in Chester. Thomas was an elderly, childless widower, with estates around the Welsh border and like the Denmans, his family had interests in lead mines.

Records show the family name spelled variously as Panton or Patton. Paul Panton, (1712–1797), the head of the senior branch of the Patton/Panton clan, of Bagillt and Coleshill, both townships of Holywell, had acquired Plas Gwyn through his marriage to Jane Jones in 1756. He developed wider interests, was called to the Bar and became an antiquarian as well as a successful industrialist who developed lead and coal mines, mainly in the Holywell area. Thomas Patton, on the other hand, confined his activities to the city of Chester, as a currier and banker. He had two nephews, Paul Panton, a tanner in Chester, and Charles Panton, who created many problems for Elizabeth after Thomas' death. In his will of 1789 Thomas wrote that his nephew Charles Panton had *'for some time past conducted himself so as to incur my displeasure. I do not think him a proper subject for my bounty.'* Thomas did, however, confirm the annuity for which he had already given Charles a bond. Paul Panton of Plas Gwyn was left Plas Panton in Denbighshire, while the other Paul Panton, Thomas' nephew in Chester, received an annuity of £10. Thomas left his house in Chester to his wife Elizabeth, being his residuary legatee.

Charles continued to behave in such an antagonistic manner towards Elizabeth that his prospects were not improved in Thomas' next will of 1790. Thomas left to his wife and her heirs property once owned by the Denmans in Llwynegrinin the parish of Mold in the county of Flint which had been bought back for her by Thomas shortly before his death. The rest of his considerable property was left her only for her lifetime, including the property at Plas Panton assigned in his previous will to Paul of Plas Gwyn. The provisions made for the disposition of these properties after his wife's death indicate Thomas' enduring personal hostility to his nephew Charles, which did not extend to any sons Charles might have. Meanwhile, as long as he had none *'but was still capable of having such,'* trustees were to administer the estate for the benefit of a long list of family members. Should sons be born to Charles they were to inherit in order of seniority, always excluding Charles himself. It is scarcely surprising that Charles should contest the will but accounts of the dispute leave considerable uncertainty as to whether Elizabeth was a wicked shrew and a bully, as Charles did not scruple to suggest, or a hard-working, virtuous widow, ensuring that her husband's wishes be respected.

Elizabeth applied for probate through her proctor, Mr Hostage, in September 1791 and in that Michaelmas Term Charles entered a list of interrogatories to witnesses concerning the making of Thomas' will. The replies made by the witnesses and entered in October 1791 indicate that the will had been properly drawn up and witnessed. John Monk gave evidence on Thomas' state of mind, deposing that he went to the office of William Hall, attorney and Town Clerk, and that '*Thomas Patton was of sound disposing mind, memory and understanding, having made Elizabeth Patton sole executor and residuary legatee.*' Samuel Williams, clerk for some years past in William Hall's office, gave his view that he knew Thomas Patton deceased and that he wrote the said will from a draft given him by Mr Hall or Mr Whiteley, Deputy Town Clerk. John Gregory, writer to Mr William Hall, also stated that Mr Thomas Patton wrote his name on the document and published and acclaimed the same as his last will and testament and was of sound and disposing mind. He did not know where the draft was but supposed it to be in his master's custody. This witness also rejected the suggestion that there was any fraud, force or contrivance on the deceased to execute the will nor did he believe that deceased would act contrary to his own disposition nor be so controlled by his wife as to act contrary to his own understanding. He said that Mrs Patton did not know the contents of the will until after the deceased was dead.

Possibly frustrated by these decided negatives to his questions, in November 1791 Charles made further colourful allegations, many concerning Elizabeth's character. He described his relationship with his uncle, claiming that Thomas always had great affection for himself and for his late father, Charles Panton, Thomas' brother, but that Thomas '*durst not speak his mind to his acquaintance.*' Charles related that thirty years ago when he was five years old Thomas took him from his mother to adopt him and bring him up as his own son. He was enrolled as Thomas' apprentice as a currier but '*not with a view to his following this trade but to prevent him being balloted to serve in the militia embodied for the city and county of Chester.*' When he finished his apprenticeship he often asked Thomas for some situation in life but was told that all the property was entailed on himself so that there was no need for him to earn his living.

Around 1785, Charles said, Thomas met Elizabeth Jones and '*was induced to marry her*' though he did not engage in his second marriage from '*want of affection to his nephew.*' On the contrary, so Charles continued, Thomas stopped on his way to get the marriage licence with his friend Joseph Dukes and said that he would never revoke the will leaving everything to Charles let him behave how he will, declaring *'let my right hand drop off my body if I do.'* Charles further alleged that a few days before the marriage in 1785, Thomas became grave and thoughtful as if some weighty matter oppressed him, and told his servant Mary Higginson that he had passed an uneasy night lamenting the position he had been drawn into and declared to her *'May my soul never ascend into Heaven if this act prove worse for Charles'* and Mary was to tell this to Charles. Charles in fact continued to live in his uncle's house until after the wedding, when Thomas bought and part furnished a house for him, appointed Mary Higginson to be his servant and gave Charles an annuity of £80.

Further startling allegations were made by Charles, that a few months after her marriage Elizabeth by the violence of her temper and disposition had obtained an undue superiority and control over Thomas and that *'with tears in his eyes'* Thomas said he regretted his marriage. According to Charles, Elizabeth prevented him seeing Charles and any of his friends and obtained sole management of all his affairs and concerns so that she had an undue influence on his making the will if he did make it. Thomas would let his wife have anything that she wanted. She frequently declared before Thomas' death that she would take care of the old banker's money and get Charles turned aside. During his last illness, Thomas said to his apothecary that he retained a great affection for his nephew Charles. Finally Charles estimated that at the time of his death Thomas possessed a yearly income of between three and five hundred pounds and an estate worth eight to ten thousand pounds and none of this came to him. Charles therefore prayed the court to agree with him that Thomas had died intestate and declared that he has seen no will or testament apart from the pretended last will and testament dated 28 August 1790 and also the previous pretended will of the said deceased now with the registrar of the court. As to the two previous wills made just before and after Thomas' marriage, they had been in the possession of Mr Whiteley, but he could not say whether they were now in existence. They never came to his *'sight, custody or possession.'* He was informed of them. He was the next of kin and had received nothing.

Grieving for the death of her husband, and burdened with his banking business, Elizabeth still vigorously countered Charles' offensive charges in an affidavit dated 5 March 1792. She declared that her husband made only two wills, in 1789 and 1790 and the latter was the true last will and testament and that she was the sole executrix. She agreed that her husband did formerly entertain a love for his nephew Charles Panton who, however, forfeited it many years ago by his behaviour to and abuse of his uncle. She believed that on the death of Charles Panton senior her husband did take Charles to live with him intending to bring him up and make him his heir had Charles behaved affectionately to him but asserted that Charles was apprenticed as a currier and not told that he did not need to work. In relation to her marriage she stated that she met her husband in 1783 and was asked to intermarry with him in 1785 and lived with him in the greatest harmony and mutual affection and she denied Charles' allegations about the marriage. As to the house, at her particular request the deceased furnished the house for Charles Panton and settled the annuity because he did not intend to leave him any part of his property. She did not believe that the alleged comment was made to Robert Owens, apothecary, who was an intimate friend and acquaintance of Charles Panton and her enemy. She agreed that the deceased's capital and income were as stated and that no part of them was bequeathed to his nephew. The judgment of the court on this unedifying family disagreement was given against Charles, vindicating Elizabeth Patton and granting her probate in 1792. At this date Elizabeth became owner of the house in Foregate Street and sole partner in the bank which Thomas Patton had carried on since 1783.

The house appears from the inventory to have been a many-storeyed comfortable family home as well as providing premises for the bank. The top floor is described as a garret, below which a middle garret of four rooms contained, with other furniture, servants' bedsteads, caneback chairs and a swing glass. The rooms in the attic storey below held grander bedsteads, four-poster with hangings, chests with drawers in oak and mahogany and easy chairs, and in the dressing rooms wardrobes, dressing tables and pier glasses. Downstairs again came the state storey and the drawing room with its worked map in a gilt frame, old pictures, family silhouettes and chimney ornaments. Past the clock in its mahogany case, the best staircase lead down to the tidy front parlour furnished with eight mahogany chairs and a Pembroke table and, for relaxation, a backgammon board. Below came the hall, the back parlour, the dining room, and the kitchen with its pantries and sculleries. Finally the bank is named, equipped with a large oak counter, a desk and stool, a double desk with more stools, a bookcase and an iron chest. This list of the essential tools of the private country banker's trade and the situation of the bank offices within the family home describes a way of doing business once common in several professions.

Mrs Patton's success in carrying on her husband's banking business is demonstrated in her will. She had managed to keep her considerable property despite the dangers faced by country banks over the years when she began banking. The terms of her will show that after her experience with her husband's family she was the more loyal to her own, leaving Halkyns, (originally Denman) property to her nephew John Edwards, so that it remained with her own kin. She left the bulk of her property to her daughter by her first marriage, Anne Wynne Jones. The manner in which she made this bequest and her determination that her son-in-law should not be able to make any use of her money, suggest that she had been made wary by Charles' allegations against her in the Consistory Court. Mrs Patton left the property destined for her daughter in the hands of trustees, for her son-in-law and her daughter. The money was, however, to be for her daughter's sole use even during the joint lives of the couple, the trustees paying rents etc '*into the proper hands of said daughter Anne Forester to and for her own sole and separate use*' and this money was, she insisted, '*not liable to debts or control of her husband notwithstanding her couverture.*' Elizabeth Patton thus ensured for her daughter a financial independence.

Mrs Patton's mistrust was of Anne's husband, George Townsend Forester, and not of his family as a whole, for she chose two of his relatives as trustees. Anne had married back into the landed gentry and the trustees, Robert Passingham Esq of Heathy, Dilton, Hampshire, and Townsend Ince Esq of Christieton, Cheshire, were brothers-in-law, related to the Foresters through the Bowen family of Camrose. Elizabeth Patton showed equal determination in steering her bank through the financial climate at which a less forceful personality might well have quailed. The danger was very close to home and very soon after Elizabeth took over in Foregate Street a neighbouring bank, Thomas and Hesketh, was forced to stop payment. Her courage and business acumen enabled her to weather the economic blizzard that destroyed many banks at this time. She died on 18 February 1803.

Yorkshire:

MARY RICHARDSON. Mary Holt was the youngest of the three daughters of John Holt, a prosperous ship-builder of Whitby. All three sisters and their brother John junior, were connected with banking. The eldest sister, Margaret Campion (*see Chapter 2*), founded her own bank at Whitby in 1800; Elizabeth married Joseph Atty, a banker at Stockton. Mary, the youngest, was born about 1755, and married in 1779 Christopher Richardson of Field House, Justice of the Peace and Deputy Lieutenant for North Riding 1752. Just before his marriage he opened a business as wine merchant in the recently de-consecrated St Ninian's Chapel, not surprisingly causing some scandal. In spite of this he was later able to open a bank, first listed as Clarke, Richardson and Hodgson in September 1786. Soon after this the Pease family, bankers at Hull, joined the Whitby partnership, and at both places these partnerships were able to survive the crisis of 1793 after a short suspension of payments but their joint reputation enabled them quickly to resume business.

In 1816 the bank at Whitby is listed as Richardson, Holt & Co, Christopher having taken as junior partner Mary's brother John Holt. After Christopher died in 1825 Mary took over his position as senior partner bringing the bank safely through the difficult years around that date while her brother John remained a junior partner. Her son Christopher joined the bank with his uncle John Holt after her death in 1840 until in 1846 they amalgamated with the joint stock bank of York City and County, later absorbed by the Midland Bank. Banking in Whitby illustrates two of the strengths of country banking partnerships, which brought in many family members and were involved in the main business activities of the neighbourhood. Here the Holts, Campions, Richardsons, Chapmans and Peases intermarried for many generations; they were successful as builders and shipowners, whalers and ancillary marine traders. In their sailcloth industry Robert Campion took out a patent in 1813 for making sailcloth without the use of starch.

MARY RIMINGTON. Mary Wilson was the daughter of a London merchant, whose success was such that her elder brother Henry was able in 1810 to buy the family estate of Broomhead from his second cousin's widow. This estate in Yorkshire had been given in the early thirteenth century to their ancestor Adam Wilson, a scutiger (medieval word for 'Esquire'), as a reward for gallantry in the Scottish wars. In 1784 Mary Wilson married John Rimington Esq of Hillsborough, who, in 1816, with two members of the Younge family, opened a bank in Sheffield. By 1830 John's widow Mary was senior partner in the bank with her son James, as well as William and George Younge. This family were long established in Sheffield. In 1793 John T. Younge & Co were button manufacturers and silver and plate merchants. A directory of 1845 still lists Rimington & Younge as bankers although another source gives 1843 as the date when they formed the basis of the Sheffield and Retford Banking Company. This was in its turn taken over by the Sheffield Union Banking Company, absorbed in 1901 by the Midland Bank.

Chapter Eight

Widows inheriting banks from their husbands: Midlands and Wales

Bedfordshire: **HANNAH GRANT**, *Leighton Buzzard*.
Herefordshire: **ESTHER CRUMMER**, *Kington*.
Northamptonshire: **ELIZABETH MARY WARNER COBB**, *Kettering*.
Nottinghamshire: **DOROTHY EVANS**, *Mansfield*; **ANN ELIZABETH EVANS**, *Mansfield*; **CATHERINE ANN EVANS**, *Mansfield*; **CHARLOTTE DOROTHY EVANS**, *Mansfield*; **SUSANNA MIDDLEMORE**, *Mansfield*.
Oxfordshire: **SARAH WOOTTEN-WOOTTEN**, *Oxford*.
Shropshire: **ANN BOULTON**, *Bridgnorth*; **SARAH SKEY**, *Bewdley*.
Staffordshire: **CATHERINE BARKER**, *Lichfield*; **SARAH FOWLER**, *Lee*.
Shropshire: **ANN WILKINSON**, *Broseley*.

Wales
Carmarthenshire: **ELIZABETH MARTEN**, *Carmarthen* and *Haverfordwest*.
Denbigh: **ANN WILKINSON** (*see* Shropshire *above*).
Monmouthshire: **MARY JONES**, *Abergavenny*, *Pontypool*.

Bedfordshire:
HANNAH GRANT. Hannah was born on 23 November 1760 into a Quaker family, the daughter of William and Mary Brook of Leighton Buzzard where her father was a prosperous wool-stapler. Hannah's mother Mary, though she had gone through several transitions on her way to becoming a Quaker, showed herself eventually as a notable supporter of the Society of Friends. Her parents, William and Mary Brotherton of Woodstock, near Oxford, though themselves members

of the Church of England, unaccountably sent her to be brought up in Warwick by a strict Presbyterian aunt. She rejoined the Church of England later, while living with her mother, Hannah's grandmother, in the Oxfordshire village of Hook Norton, but perhaps harking back to her non-conformist upbringing, she became, in 1753, in her late twenties, a convinced Quaker. She married Joseph Brook six years later and settled at Leighton Buzzard in a strong community of Friends. The Brooks offered their home for the monthly meeting in 1773 so that the local Friends did not have to walk the seven miles to Hogstyend in Woburn. Mary Brook *'appeared very acceptably in the ministry'* and for many years preached all over the country and wrote many influential pamphlets which were frequently reprinted and translated into many languages. She was *'a sincere Friend of exemplary life and conversation'* and *'an affectionate wife and a tender mother.'* Her first daughter Hannah lived to the great age of ninety-three, but her only other child born two years later, in 1862, died aged only a few months.

In 1780 Hannah married another Quaker, John Grant, a tallow chandler, a corn factor and grocer. He was an enterprising business man, greatly involved in Quaker good works. In 1786 he bought property in North Street and pulled down some cottages in order to build a new Meeting House. It was registered as a dissenting place of worship in 1789. The Quaker community grew and in 1807 John Grant bought some adjoining land as a burying ground. The first person to be buried there was Thomas Bradshaw, a former naval captain who had been converted to Quakerism by the preaching of Hannah's mother, Mary Brook, whom he heard when he chanced out of curiosity to walk into the Meeting House. Leaving the navy, he and his wife became the reading master and matron at the Friends' boarding school at Ackworth from 1791 until they retired in 1804. Returning south to Leighton Buzzard they were cared for in their old age by Hannah Grant. Life as John Grant's wife may at times have been difficult for Hannah, for John, in spite of his Quaker beliefs, was easily provoked to anger and controversy. In 1796 he was accused of profiteering by monopolising essential foodstuffs to increase their price. He defended himself vigorously in an aggrieved and petulant pamphlet addressed to the 'inhabitants' of Leighton Buzzard offering to pay £100 to the poor if anyone could prove the allegation. He claimed to have sold his entire stock of wheat to the local baker as soon as it was threshed, and that in any case most of his dealings were in horse corn.

In 1810 John Grant joined the recently formed partnership of William Exton and John Dollin Bassett to take over the ailing firm of Wickers Hodges, straw hat manufacturers, including their stock in trade. The difficulties they met in regaining profitability suggested the need for formal local banking. They were joined in 1812 by two other prominent Quakers, Peter Bassett and Joseph Sharples to found the Leighton Buzzard bank. John Grant took into partnership as corn, coal and timber merchants and wharfingers, William Exton as well as Edward Lawford, the son of his widowed sister. Her husband, a poor clergyman, had died leaving her with children to support. John Grant's wharf was near a bridge over the Grand Junction canal; he also owned a grocer's shop in North Street near the Meeting House. He and Hannah lived at the bottom of the High Street near Church Square, not far from the bank which had opened in the front room of 38 High Street. Their only child, also Hannah, married Francis Darby, of the Coalbrookdale iron founding and banking family. (*See Chapter 2*)

In 1812 an extension to the Meeting House was built on land given by John Grant. All this land was handed over to Quaker trustees when John Grant died in 1842. He had also taken a prominent part in other good works in the town in promoting education for poor children. In 1813 with John Dollin Bassett and other non-conformists they established two schools for boys and girls run on the new monitorial system promoted by Joseph Lancaster. This idea had been developed by Dr Andrew Bell, an Anglican cleric in the service of the East India Company. In England it was taken up by Joseph Lancaster, a Quaker. In 1810 he and his friends formed the Royal Lancastrian Association which changed its name in 1814 to the British and Foreign School Society which drew its main support from dissenters. In 1811 the Anglicans formed their own society, the National Society for Educating the Poor in the Principles of the Established Church. This proved so successful that they eventually had more schools than the dissenters over the country as a whole. By 1815 these schools in Leighton Buzzard were attended by 192 boys and 212 girls in the daytime and 147 boys and 110 girls in the evening. There was also a Sunday school for adults.

An early responsibility of the new bank was to be one of the six Bedfordshire banks chosen in 1816 to take part in issuing new silver coins. This brought in many new customers among whom were not only prominent merchants and professional people but members of the local gentry. The bank was well funded; the five original partners had each contributed £1,600 making a total stock of £8,000. Peter Bassett died in 1821 leaving his share to his son John Dollin Bassett who therefore owned two of the five shares. In 1827 the partnership split up. It was well known that John Grant and William Exton were continually having public disagreements so that Exton and Sharples took over the branches at Hitchin and Luton while Grant and John Dollin Bassett remained in charge at Leighton Buzzard. About this time, in 1831, John's *'questionable accounting'* and his stubborn refusal to take advice was referred to the Yearly Meeting. In 1836 John Dollin Bassett's son Peter was brought into the partnership though not yet twenty-one because of John Grant's incompetence, in spite of his objections. This arrangement lasted for the next six years until John Grant died on 29 December 1842. He appointed as executors his widow Hannah, his daughter Hannah Darby, his son-in-law Francis Darby, his grandson Abraham Darby and great-nephew William Grant. Hannah Grant took over her husband's partnership in the bank with John Dollin Bassett and his sons Peter and Francis, and continued as an active partner until her death aged ninety-three in 1853. The bank continued successfully to serve the community for more than forty years until it merged with Barclays in 1896.

Herefordshire:
ESTHER CRUMMER. Esther Davies, who as Mrs Esther Crummer was to spend many years as partner in the Kington and Radnorshire bank, came from an unassuming Welsh family, who, however, like many from Wales, could trace their forebears back through several generations of Radnorshire farmers. She was born in 1783, the daughter of Thomas William Davies of Bronlys and other property in Radnorshire, and her mother was Esther Powell who was thirty-one at the time of her wedding in 1767. As the bridegroom was only twenty-three the marriage may have been arranged between two neighbouring families for dynastic reasons. Among the children of the forty-six-year union were James, Esther and William. The latter remained very close to his roots, married Sarah

Thomas and became a doctor in Brecon. Unlike his brother James left Wales in 1790, aged only thirteen and was apprenticed to the Kington attorneys, Harries and Cheese. About the same time Edmund Cheese, a land owner at Lyonshall, who had married his partner's daughter, took their son Edmund, in his early twenties, into the firm. Edmund Cheese junior married Mary Watkins, daughter of a Welsh neighbour.

James Davies, having reached his majority, opened his own firm of attorneys in 1799 and for good measure took over the management of the local stage coaches too. Not content with these activities, in 1808 he joined Edmund Cheese junior in founding the Kington and Radnorshire bank. The third partner in the new bank, James Crummer, was in due course to bring Esther Davies into the business world. The three founding partners each placed a sum of money into his own private account with the bank. The bank, unusually, had no capital for although a draft agreement was drawn up it was left blank, the partners apparently enjoying perfect confidence in the probity of all. James Crummer, an outsider among these border families, had come from Ireland, the son of Christopher Crummer, a Protestant, of Ballina, a fishing port and market town in County Mayo. From this background, in his early thirties, James brought his expertise with horses and cattle, as well as his complement of Irish charm, to London. In 1780 he secured a respectable, if not at first a very lucrative, position as land agent and steward at Berington Hall (now owned, since 2007, by the National Trust) near Leominster, which the Honourable Thomas Harley, MP for Herefordshire, had bought some twenty years earlier. Harley, after consulting Capability Brown about the garden, rebuilt the house from Henry Holland's plans. The Harleys were wealthy, for Thomas Harley's father, the Earl of Oxford and Mortimer, and Chancellor of the Exchequer, was one of the promoters of the South Sea Company. Thomas prospered as a London merchant, becoming Lord Mayor in 1767 at the age of thirty-seven. He also acted as agent for pay and clothing for the British army in America.

At Berington Hall, Crummer, as steward, occupied an office with living rooms above and his own door out to a courtyard. The salary at £52. 10s was scarcely lavish even had it been paid regularly, but this did not in fact happen for the next eighteen years, after which the deficit was paid with interest. Luckily during these years James had found other sources of income, taking five per cent on transactions as land agent for several clients, including the famous industrialists and inventors Matthew Boulton and James Watt father and son. James Crummer not only acted as steward for their estates in the counties of Hereford, Brecon and Radnor, but also became a personal friend of their families. James Watt junior was a trustee for the settlement at the Crummer's marriage. In 1811 James Crummer enjoyed a prominent position locally, as magistrate, trustee for the turnpike roads, and eventually as High Sheriff of Radnorshire in 1820. Some years earlier, at Thomas Harley's death in 1804, his daughter Lady Rodney, having inherited his estates in trust for her son found James Crummer indispensable as her steward. When James Crummer joined in founding the Kington bank in 1808 he bought a farm-house near Llandrindod Wells which he improved and named Howey Hall. In politics he supported John Lubbock when he stood as Parliamentary candidate for Leominster, perhaps partly to support a member of the family which acted as London agents for the Kington bank.

James Crummer was sixty-three when in 1811 he married the twenty-eight-year-old Esther, sister of his partner James Davies. From their marriage settlement it appears that Esther was the major contributor; she brought '£4,000 *or thereabouts*' to be paid to James Crummer for his own use, his trustees being James Watt and David Lloyd. James Crummer brought £1,253 together with the landed property consisting of Howey Hall, '*the capital messuage, buildings, farm and lands in the parish of Disserth near Llandrindod.*' The income from the tenancies was to go to James Crummer and after his death to his widow, Esther, who was to pay her parents £500 a year for their lifetime. Her trustees were her brother James Davies and Thomas Frankland Lewis. The family seat of the Hon Thomas Frankland Lewis, Harpton Court, was not far from Kington. Thomas succeeded his father in 1797 entering Parliament for a remote constituency of Beaumaris in Anglesey in 1812 and served for that borough in three succeeding Parliaments and also for Radnor. He was appointed Privy Counsellor in 1827 and Secretary of the Treasury and Vice President of the Board of Trade. He became one of the Poor Law Commissioners, resigning in 1838 when his son George succeeded him in this office. Esther was fortunate in having a trustee with not inconsiderable influence. She seems not to have had a striking presence herself. In the long drawing room at Ridgebourne, Esther Crummer's home, with its large windows framing views of the quiet Herefordshire countryside, hangs her portrait. She is wearing a large black velvet hat over which nod four tall white ostrich feathers. She is shown sitting in an armchair draped with furs and lace so that the artist seems more impressed by her elegant possessions than her personality. Nevertheless, she retains a formidable reputation. At her wedding in Bronllys her family may well have considered that her husband's position in the bank, his useful connections at Berington and his Irish charm more than outweighed the considerable disparity in their ages.

The portrait of Esther Crummer

The Crummers lived very comfortably, using Howey Hall for their holidays, enjoying the pump room at Llandrindod Wells, while in Kington they lived in Hollyday House, near the bank. They were also close to Ridgebourne House, the home of Edmund Cheese junior and later of his son Edmund Watkins Cheese, both James' partners in the bank. From Berington, Lady Rodney continued to consult James, and occasionally Esther, on estate problems. Esther and James, who were childless, did not have many years together before James' eyes began to give him serious trouble. At that date a cataract operation would at best have involved a long, painful and worrying illness. In the event, James' operation went very wrong indeed and he was tormented by the series of gruesome treatments that followed. The sea bathing at Tenby and Aberystwyth that was prescribed in 1820 must have offered a welcome cessation of visits to the London surgeons, but he died the following year.

After James' death Esther moved from Hollyday House to Castlefield House in Kington, but only four years later she must have been further distressed by a very public disagreement with James Cheese, whose family she would have considered as friends and colleagues. In 1825 he posted a bill stating that Esther Crummer had refused to give back the house she rented from him, and that she had called in constables to prevent him from taking possession. She must have been pleased when she was able finally to move in 1838 to Ridgebourne House, which her brother James had bought on the death of Edmund Watkins Cheese. As its name suggests, the house is built on the hills a little above the town. Originally a seventeenth century farm house, Ridgebourne had in 1806 been dignified by Edmund Cheese with the addition of a marble Italianate villa frontage. Esther's household was managed in considerable comfort, with a December butcher's bill including three stone of beef '*for self and small staff.*' Intriguingly, the accounts one January mention 12 oranges for 1/6*d* and 4 lemons for 8*d*, 12 lb sugar for 5/-, 12 lb lump sugar for 6/6*d* and 4 lb caster sugar for 1/10*d*. Marmalade might have been planned; but the accounts continue with 1lb mustard for 1/8*d* and a quarter lb white pepper, which would make an unusual recipe. As for other domestic duties expected of a housewife, Esther brewed the ale and beer for the household and made wine from gooseberries, currants, elderberries and raspberries, and may have fortified the wine with the brandy she bought.

Throughout the years of keeping house Esther continued her partnership in the bank which she took over on her husband's death in 1821, and whose scope she and her partners, with the addition of a connection of hers, David Oliver, enlarged in 1838 by opening a branch in Knighton. In a directory of 1851 Esther is listed, among the Clergy and Gentry, as Banker, though her diary entries during these years are domestic and social, without reference to business matters. Comparison with the diaries kept by her great-nephew when he was a partner in the bank shows that he, too, kept his entries for home matters without mention of his work at the bank. This was, presumably, for men and women partners alike, something not to be associated with the social world of the drawing room. Esther's health was not robust and she frequently resorted to spa bathing for its improvement, usually at Llandrindod but sometimes further afield, spending six weeks at Aix-la-Chapelle in 1847.

In spite of her poor health Esther remained involved in the bank for more than 30 years, being named in a partnership deed of 1857. She died in January the following year. Esther's brother James, also childless, had died two years earlier, and his will left half his estate to her absolutely and the other half to be distributed at her discretion to their three great-nephews, the children of their late niece Esther, daughter of their brother William. The younger Esther had married Richard Banks, son of Lawrence of Boys Hall, near Ashford, Kent, whose family, living in a house with capacious cellars, on the Knatchbulls' Kentish estate, enjoyed the distinction of being generally known as the Knatchbulls' smuggling managers. The third great-nephew, William Lawrence Banks, inherited Esther's father's property at Bronllys, in Radnorshire. To the second great-nephew James Banks, in Holy Orders, she left half of James Davies' residuary legacy, as well as the house at Moorcourt. Additionally, a lump sum was left to his wife Marianne.

James Banks subsequently took James Davies' name. The eldest great-nephew, Richard William Banks, inherited the main bulk of her property and the Kington bank. He married Rosa Hartland and their son William Hartland Banks continued the association with

Ridgebourne, building a grander house on land next to the old house. He became a partner in the bank, later indulging in his interests in photography and landscaping the magnificent gardens at Hergist Croft. The bank operated successfully for more than 100 years as a private partnership until they were absorbed in 1910 by the Metropolitan Banking Company, subsequently part of the Midland Bank.

Northamptonshire:

ELIZABETH MARY WARNER COBB. Elizabeth's marriage to James Cobb was followed by the birth of their first child, Sarah, in 1787. Sarah's burial in 1864 is the only mention of the Cobb family recorded in the parish church registers, so it is likely that the family were originally non-conformist. This adherence is supported by an incident noted in the Kettering Vestry records for 1831. Mrs Cobb was fined £2. 16s for non-payment of the church rate, a protest made by many conscientious dissenters; on the other hand her husband, James Cobb, was a member of the Church of England. In 1786 James Cobb was an ironmonger and manufacturer of boots for the army. With him in this enterprise were his partners James Benton, Thomas Gotch and John Keep, a tinman, brazier and stock farmer, the ironmongery providing nails and the farm the hides for the army boots.

By 1792 James Cobb and his partners had opened the Kettering bank and in 1797 he retired from the boot factory. At that date he took on a further commitment through being accepted on to the committee of the Kettering Vestry on which he was to serve for the next five years. The Kettering bank, under the sole name of James Cobb, appears in the bank lists of 1797 and 1799 and as J. Cobb & Co. in Holden's directory of 1802. Gotch sources suggest that James Cobb was a sleeping partner in the boot factory and no more active in the bank. Thomas Gotch considered the bank as his *'financial tributary'* to which he had *'allied himself'* to ensure *'a free flow of capital between the two concerns.'* The bank was soon known in Kettering as Keep, Gotch, Cobb & Benton though the name Keep is not nationally listed until the 1800 *Post Office Directory*, and Thomas Gotch does not appear as a banker until the reference to his death and replacement in the bank by his son John Cooper Gotch in the *London Gazette* of 1806 (page 285). Evidence that James Cobb died in 1802 when he last appeared in the directories as a partner in the bank is supported by the fact that his name last appears in the records of the *Kettering Vestry Minutes* at that date.

It is probable that Elizabeth took over the bank partnership on her husband's death; she is recorded as retiring in the same London Gazette of 1806 in which John Cooper Gotch took over from his father. In 1807, after Elizabeth had retired, James Cobb's executor, Timothy Cobb, of Banbury, presumably a relative and possibly connected with the Banbury banker of that name, separated the accounts of the bank and the boot factory and settled the debts owed by the boot and shoe business to James Cobb's estate. The bank continued to flourish under John Cooper Gotch until his death in 1852 when the bank was taken on by his son Thomas Henry Gotch, while the boot manufacture was continued by his son John Davis Gotch.

The bank failed in 1857 due to rash advances to a Revd Macpherson who was allowed to borrow £46,000 without collateral for an enterprising but unfortunately unsuccessful project, to add peat to night soil to make field manure. The failure also involved the boot factory and John Davis Gotch, who remained an undischarged bankrupt until 1861. In 1857 Gotch properties were sold, including the bank premises in the Market Place where Elizabeth Cobb had made her home since the 1820s. Nevertheless when Sarah Cobb died in 1864 she was still living in the house in Market Place which had belonged to her mother. Chesham House, the Gotch family home and their shoe warehouse combined, the currier's shop, tan-yards as well as three farms and eleven cottages had also been sold. The recovery from this failure showed how members of a strong non-conformist network could retrieve their fortunes. By 1863 the Gotch brothers were once again in business as manufacturers and in less than ten years, by 1871, had become the largest employers of labour in the town, in which remarkable recovery it is likely that their respected position in the Baptist church had provided a guarantee.

Nottinghamshire:
DOROTHY EVANS, executor/partner, widow of Francis Evans;
ANN, CATHERINE, CHARLOTTE EVANS, executors/partners, daughters of Francis Evans; **SUSANNA MIDDLEMORE**, executor/partner, widow of William Richard Middlemore.

The Mansfield bank is first listed as Moore and Co in 1804, the partners in 1810 being George Moore, Thomas Maltby, Francis Evans and William Richard Middlemore. By 1816 the latter two had died and the partnership was accordingly dissolved. The executors of Francis Evans were his widow Dorothy and his three daughters Catherine, Ann and Charlotte. Susanna (spelt in different ways but thus on her tombstone) was listed as widow and executrix for William Richard Middlemore. She and her husband lived at Orston Hall, which remained her home until she died in 1849; she is buried there beside her husband in the church to which she was devoted and had given the organ. The Middlemores were connected with the ancient family of that name at Haselwell Hall in Kings Norton in Worcestershire. Susanna was the daughter of John Matthews of Tynemouth and connected through General Matthews with the Burdons, bankers at Berwick and Newcastle on Tyne. The Mansfield bank continued successfully until purchased in 1871 by Samuel Smith & Co of Nottingham.

Oxfordshire:

SARAH WOOTTEN-WOOTTEN. The Wootten (some sources spell in Wooten) family had many business interests in the city of Oxford and neighbouring parishes including Wootten's Brewery in St Clements which was later taken over by Halls in 1896. Richard Wootten was also a mercer and his shop in Oxford's High Street is still listed in 1823 in the *Piggott's Directory for Oxford*. The Undershells had come from Bermondsey and William Undershell (later Wootten) was listed as a banker's clerk age 21 in the 1841 census. He was living with his grandfather, Richard Wootten, the retired Mayor of Oxford, banker, etc.

Sarah Wootten Wootten (some sources hyphenate the name) was born Sarah Parker in Oxford in 1823 and baptised in July of that year in the church of St Peter's-in-the-East. She was the daughter of Elizabeth and William Parker, print seller, of High Street Oxford. In December 1850 Sarah was married in Iffley by the Rev Thomas Evetts to William Wootten Undershell. He later took the name surname of Wootten thus becoming William Wootten Wootten. Sarah is recorded as being included as a partner in Wootten's Bank at the age of 65 on the death of her husband in 1887, although she is not listed in the 1888 *Banking*

Almanac. As well as the partnership Sarah inherited her husband's brewery in St Clements (previously Wootten and Cole) which she sold in 1891, subsequently taken over by Halls Brewery. She also inherited her married home Headington House and the house that they owned for letting, namely Headington Lodge (later White Lodge). She gave this is 1888 to her son Montague on his marriage. He and his wife Mary and their son Kenneth lived there until Montague's disastrous death. In 1920 it was bought from Montague Wootten Wootten's estate by Edwin J Hall, who lived in Clifton House on the London Road at Headington who built the cinema in New High Street in his garden.

In 1855 the Oxford Bank was known as Undershell's Bank and the partners were John Undershell and William Wootten Wootten, but by 1883 it was known as Wootten's Bank. Sarah died in 1904 and in 1909 when the sole surviving partner was her son Montague William Wootten Wootten, the bank was acquired by Barclay and Company Limited. The *History of Headington* states that in the same year Montague Wootten committed suicide in his house Headington Lodge as "a result of financial problems." He was a partner of Parsons Thomson & Co. (Barclays) The Old Bank, High Street, Oxford, now a hotel.

Shropshire:

ANN BOULTON. Ann Sparrye, born about 1750, married Joseph Boulton, the son of Job and Johanna Boulton in May 1772 at St Mary Magdalene, Bridgnorth. He was born in November 1743. During the first 16 years of their marriage they had nine children, though their first child died within a few days. Grey Edward, Mary Ann, Sophia, Joseph, Thomas, John, Charlotte and Elizabeth were born by 1788. Joseph, a mercer and draper in the town and one of His Majesty's Justices of the Peace for Shropshire, had added banking to his activities by 1783, with William Bates, an alderman who was also his partner in the drapery, and a friend who stood witness at his marriage. The bank continued successfully though Joseph's health began to decline. He lived to see his daughter Sophia married at the end of 1795, to Phillip Palmer Esq of East Bridgford, Nottinghamshire, but soon afterwards went to Bath in the hope that the waters would restore his health. Sadly, he died there early in 1796, leaving his wife to care for their children and also to take his place in the bank, together with their old friend William Bates. She also carried on the business of mercer, draper and wool-stapler and proprietor of the Hampton Iron Lode company.

By the time of her husband's death, though Elizabeth, her youngest child, was only eight, her older sons were well on the way to independence. It is unusual that none of her children took an interest in banking. Grey Edward, who had been enrolled in the *Burgess Book* in 1794, had, however, entered the mercery business and was joined there by his younger brother Thomas. Joseph junior was studying to be a surgeon. Finding her children so successful in their chosen careers, Ann Boulton, though only middle-aged, decided to retire from banking and all her other enterprises. On 31 March 1803 she handed over the bank to William Bates as senior partner. At the same time William Jones was added to the partnership and the two men carried on the bank until it failed in 1816. In the event, it was fortunate for the family that the younger Boultons had confined themselves to Ann's other interests. Grey Edward made such a success of the mercery that with his profits he was able to acquire a nearby estate, joining the local landed gentry. Grey Edward's son Phillip John, enrolled as a burgess in 1830, left Bridgnorth and the estate to become a successful merchant in London. The next brother, Joseph junior, enrolled in the Bridgnorth Burgesses Book in 1801, under the heading 'Residence at Time of Enrolment' which is given as London and under 'In what Right Enrolled' the reason is given as 'another son.' Joseph had successfully completed his medical training and had by 1815 set up practice as a surgeon in London. Meanwhile, remaining in Bridgnorth, her son Thomas, a burgess in 1803 and having succeeded his brother Grey Edward, in the mercery, was enterprising enough to advertise in 1821 that he was in London *'selecting the most fashionable articles for dress which will be offered for inspection'* to his Bridgnorth customers.

Although successful mainly as entrepreneurs, the Boulton family were also branching out into wider spheres. John, Ann's youngest son, a burgess in 1804, joined the navy at this critical period in the defence of the country. Ann's grandson William, supported by his father, Thomas' mercery, took his BA degree at Christ Church, Oxford, and as his enrolment in the Burgess Book in 1830 shows, was still in residence pursuing his academic career there at that date completing his Master's degree, which he took in 1831. He was headmaster of Wem Grammar School for nearly forty years, from 1839 to 1878.

Shropshire:

Sarah Skey. When Sarah Laurens Bicknell, a London girl, married Samuel Skey in December 1800, she became the second wife of a country gentleman and step-mother to three girls. Her father was the solicitor to the Admiralty and Navy, with an office in Chancery Lane and a house in Spring Gardens Terrace. This move took her from the life of the metropolis to that of a small country town where she was able to take on many new responsibilities. Her husband, aged forty-one, was the owner of Spring Grove, Wribbenhall, between Kidderminster and Bewdley, where he was a banker. The house had a romantic history, the site having been marked down by Samuel's father when he was a struggling young man, who resolved to build his house there one day. Having received a legacy from a relative in Upton on Severn he began manufacturing chemicals, later making brass and pewter ware and with the proceeds succeeded in building his house in Spring Grove. By 1782 Samuel's father had also opened a bank in Bewdley, with Wilson A. Roberts, Jonathan Skey and Samuel Kenrick.

Another branch of the Skey family carried on several businesses at Upton on Severn; James Skey, father and son, and Thomas Brockhurst were bankers and ironmongers there in 1792, and later opened a brewery. Samuel II, Sarah's husband, died in March 1806, still only in his forties, but in the course of their short married life he and Sarah had three sons. Thus, on Samuel's death Sarah was left with their three very young children, of whom the youngest, Arthur, had been born only two months before his father's death. The eldest son, Samuel, only five years old, inherited the estate. Charles, her second son, died while still a baby, so when in 1812 her eleven-year-old Samuel, also died, Sarah was left with only their third son, Arthur, then six years old, to succeed. Meanwhile Sarah also had charge of the three daughters—now approaching marriageable age—of Samuel's first wife Mary Divett. Caroline the youngest, did not marry. Mary, the eldest, (co-heiress) married in 1814 William Burton, son of Sir Charles Burton Bart of Pollerton, Co Carlow. One of her sons was named for her father Samuel Skey and another joined the army and became *aide de camp* to the king of Bavaria.

The second daughter, Louisa, also married well, into a family with whom the Skeys were already connected, James Taylor (1783-1852) of Moseley Hall and Bordesley Hall. James inherited these estates from his father, John Taylor, who had married Louisa's aunt, also Sarah Skey, unashamedly described as *'a rich heiress.'* The Taylors were partners in the flourishing Birmingham bank Taylor, Lloyds and also button manufacturers, perhaps with brass from the Skey foundry. Although some of the Taylors were Quakers, James Taylor was a strict Unitarian but in spite of his credentials for not being a typical landowner and manufacturer, both his houses were attacked and destroyed by the mob in the Birmingham riots of 1791.

Sarah may well have helped her sister Maria make a less conventional but more romantic marriage. In 1800 John Constable, then aged twenty-four, met Maria Bicknell when she was only twelve years old. Art critics suggest that the love he came to feel for her proved to be the catalyst for his painting. Be that as it may, John and Maria struggled through the parental disapproval but were fortunate in having the support of Maria's sister Sarah. John was able to continue his courtship of Maria while she was staying with Sarah at Spring Grove and eventually was able to marry her in 1816. Her father's final approval can be seen from the fact that he left at his death £20,000 to his son-in-law. In 1806, when her husband died, Sarah was left not only with these family responsibilities but in sole charge of the Bewdley bank, which Samuel had split off in 1790 from the original partnership as the New Bank. Although it is listed in 1812 and 1813 as Skey & Sons, Sarah is named as sole partner. At this date the Skey bank was the only one in the town to have the added responsibility of issuing its own promissory notes. Sarah Skey married secondly the Revd Joseph Fletcher, the young rector of Dowles, half a mile from Bewdley. The bank partnership continued under the same title until it closed in 1824. Samuel Skey's house and grounds at Spring Grove have become the West Midlands Safari Park.

Staffordshire:

CATHERINE BARKER. John Barker, Catherine's husband was a prominent figure in his community; whilst still in his thirties he was elected bailiff for Lichfield, and was Commissioner for the Turnpike

Trust for Lichfield and Staffordshire. He founded the Lichfield bank by 1765 in which he was the only partner at that date. John and Catherine's first child, Samuel, was born in May that same year. Samuel was followed by John, born 1767, Catherine 1770 and Edward 1772. Also in that auspicious year, 1765, John was writing to Erasmus Darwin about forming a partnership with the ironmaster Samuel Garbett and Robert Bage, the renowned paper mill owner at Elford, to make nails by building a forge and slitting mills at Wichnor, the water to come from a new cutting taken from the Trent which later became part of the Grand Trunk Canal. This enterprise, making iron nails, operated for nearly twenty years, but ended disastrously in bankruptcy. From his other business successes John Barker was able to buy Harleston Manor near Elford in 1772 from Sir John Egerton and move in with his wife and family. Towards the end of his life, he was corresponding with Matthew Boulton of Birmingham, the well-known manufacturer. Clearly his purchase of the manor and being able to describe himself in directories not only as draper and banker but also as gentleman, had by no means inclined him to retire from business in order to enjoy the gentility of a country life.

After John Barker's death in 1781 his widow carried on the bank as 'Catherine Barker,' a title which by 1793 had become 'Cath. Barker & Son' she having been joined by her eldest son Samuel, who followed his father also in local affairs as junior bailiff. One of the first tasks Catherine had to face was her husband's bankruptcy. She had to sell the Wichnor forge and mills which were by then operating at a loss. She and Samuel were able to save the bank, which survived under their management. At her death in 1803 her son retired and the bank was taken over by her husband's nephew John Barker Scott. In 1812 the bank was issuing promissory notes with John Barker Scott, the only partner. He soon took in his younger brother Robert and two others, James Palmer and William Bird. This partnership was dissolved in 1818 and the bank continued under James Palmer, joined by Richard Green until it failed in 1855.

SARAH FOWLER. Sarah Moore, the daughter of a Stafford cordwainer, was only 18 when she married John Gaunt in 1792 at St Mary's, Stafford. He was nearly 15years older than her, a merchant and button maker, though with a family tradition of descent from the famous John of Gaunt. They lived at Highfield House, the family home on the edge of Leek, where their four children were born. The Gaunts formed part of an aspiring social circle of people who had prospered enough to own houses large enough to be a Hall or House. After John Gaunt's death in 1800, Sarah married John Fowler, some twenty years her senior, who took her and her brood of small children to Horton Hall, where their daughter Phoebe Elizabeth was born in 1810.

By 1825 John Fowler had opened a bank at Leek, with a branch at Congleton, in partnership with Sarah's eldest sons, John and Matthew Gaunt. Her daughter Mary Gaunt had married Henry Charles Dakeyne, a Derbyshire gentleman whose family were connected with a bank at Darley Dale, but who lived in St John's Wood, a fashionable London suburb, and had four children. Sarah's youngest daughter, Phoebe Fowler, did not involve herself in the bank, but married Fitzjames Watt of Morisbrooke and also had four children. By 1829, after her husband's death, Sarah had become senior partner and carried on the bank with her elder sons until her death at the age of seventy-two in 1846. Unfortunately for her sons, in the following year a robbery at T. Rogers, their London agents, caused them to withdraw support from their country correspondent banks. The Congleton branch first, and subsequently the Leek bank, stopped payment; Rogers themselves failing a little later. Sarah's eldest son John, never in good health, died before his younger brother Matthew, who consequently inherited Highfield House. He was still there, as present representative of the family, a J.P. and barrister in 1847. He had presumably succeeded in paying the debts of the bank, or his manor would have become the property of the creditors under the terms of unlimited liability.

Shropshire:

ANN WILKINSON, executor/partner. Ann Wilkinson is listed in one source in both the Midlands and in Wales. This source, Leekey's list of bankers of 1813 exceptionally includes in the column headed 'Bank Title' two iron works. Ann Wilkinson appears as an executor for her husband at Brymbo Iron Works, Denbigh, and at Bradley Iron Works, Staffs. Her husband John had founded the Broseley bank in 1800 but by 1810 the *Post Office Directory* gives only '*executors of,*' unnamed, under the Broseley bank. It has been assumed that John Wilkinson was a partner in the two iron works as well as in the Broseley bank and it appears likely that his widow was one of the unnamed executors in the bank in 1810. In 1814 the Broseley bank closed without loss to the public.

Wales—Carmarthenshire:

ELIZABETH MARTEN. When John Marten, partner in the Union Bank of Carmarthen and Haverfordwest died intestate in September 1810 his widow Elizabeth took over as senior partner in the bank. She was no stranger to that countryside or its people as her father, John Lewes Phillips, was vicar of St Clere's (now Clears) and she had grown up in this village on the road between Haverfordwest and Carmarthen, rather nearer the latter, on the estuary of Afon Cynin. Her grandfather, John Adams Esq of Whitland, and her first husband, whom she married in 1794, Walter Powell Esq of Maesgwynne were from local landowning families. Elizabeth had three children, Walter Rice Howell Powell, the heir, and two daughters. Her younger sister Charlotte also enlarged the family connections locally by her marriage in 1800 to John Lord, whose mother was the daughter of Sir John Owen, 3rd Bart of Orielton, Pembrokeshire. The title became extinct but John Lord, having been left the estate by his kinsman Hugh, 6th Bart, took the name and arms of Owen and was created baronet in 1813. He became Lord Lieutenant and MP for Pembrokeshire and Governor of Milford Haven and their son Hugh, Elizabeth's nephew, born 1803, became the heir.

Elizabeth's second husband, John Marten, had been a banker since 1796; Marten & Co. were listed in subsequent directories until 1811. However, an indenture, dated 19 June 1802, does not put John Marten first of the partners; it lists John Bateman, Gent. of Haverfordwest, of the first part, John Marten Esq, Thomas Waters the Elder of Treventy, near St Clere's and Herbert Lloyd Gent. of Carmarthen of the second part and Thomas Bowen of the third part. The equity is described; the capital was to be three thousand pounds, one thousand from John Bateman one thousand jointly from John Marten, Thomas Waters and Herbert Lloyd and one thousand from Thomas Bowen, the profits to be distributed in proportion. The business was to be carried on from the latter's house in

Haverfordwest for a term of seventeen years and six months. They were to be joint traders and bankers from Haverfordwest and with unusual ambition also to the cities of London and Bristol. Provincial bankers found it important to engage with an agent in London, but in this instance an extra agency in Bristol also made good geographic sense.

Elizabeth took over her late husband's original partners and brought in Thomas Waters junior, whose family came from her father's parish of St Clere's. They were all listed in the covenant of 14 January 1811 between the administratrix, named as Elizabeth Marten of Laugharne, '*widow of the late John Marten Esq, deceased of the same place and Messrs Bateman, Waters the Elder, Lloyd, Waters the Younger, of Fountain Hall, Carmarthen, Bowen and John Mathias.*' Although the covenants refer to Haverfordwest the bank also traded in Carmarthen while the licence of 1813 to issue its own promissory notes is for Carmarthenshire rather than for either of these towns. Elizabeth Marten is not named among the partners on the bank notes. The licence was presumably applied for after John Marten's death and before his widow signed the partnership deed as administratrix. Elizabeth dissolved the partnership in 1814 and retired, leaving the original partnership with the addition of John Stacey. The bank ceased as Mathias, Lloyd & Bowen at Haverfordwest that year, John Mathias and Thomas Bowen becoming bankrupt in 1816. In Carmarthen, as Waters, Jones & Co., the bank continued until it failed in 1831. The note issue which by 1825, ten years after Elizabeth's death, had become over-extended to £100,000 through massive advances to cattle drovers, though reduced by 1831 to £70,000 (still considered by clients as too adventurous) undoubtedly precipitated the bankruptcy.

The families in these partnerships were typical of the mix of community representatives who combined to operate so many country banks. The Mathias family were merchants and maltsters and a William Mathias had been in partnership in another bank, that of Phillips & Co. in Haverfordwest as far back as 1793 and John Bateman was an attorney. Even more typically, many of the partners in these banks came from the local landowners. The Martens had their house at Laugharne, the Waters lived at St Clere's where they must have been long acquainted with Elizabeth and her father, the rector there. Thomas Waters traced a connection with the Sir Richard Waters who was the father of Lucy Waters, a favourite at the court of Charles II. This combination of trades, professions and gentry, often with a dash of something out of the ordinary in their background, usually appears as a source of strength in country banking so the enterprise handed on by Elizabeth Marten seems to have been exceptionally unfortunate.

Denbighshire: *see* **ANN WILKINSON**, Staffordshire.

Monmouthshire:

MARY JONES. Mary Jones, the other widow banking in Wales, and her husband John, who was her first cousin, also came from landowning families. The estates owned by Mary's father, Richard Lee, were at Clytha and Llanfoist, near Abergavenny, and also in Kent, at Great Delce. The Lees of Great Delce, Kent, were connected, through the Kentish Wyborns of Hawkwell Place, Kent, with Catherine Bradley, banker in Sandwich. Catherine Wyborn married Phillip Jones, and was the mother of John Jones. Mary Lee married John Jones in 1789, spending many years in rearing a fine family of thirteen children. When her husband died in 1828, just short of their ruby wedding anniversary, he had been a senior partner of the Abergavenny bank for some fifteen years, a steadying influence on a business which had had a somewhat Dickensian start. The founder, Sir Robert Salusbury Bart, had entered the Jones family partnership in 1801 before running up such a burden of debt that by 1816 he found himself a prisoner in the King's Bench. On John's death, his eldest son John succeeded to the estates, while Mary took over the senior partnership in the bank, in which their second son Philip, of Hill House, Abergavenny, and Perthyre House, near Monmouth, was already a partner. Not content with operating the Abergavenny bank only, they opened another in Pontypool, which later had a branch in Monmouth. Mary and her son were both still partners when they accepted the offer of amalgamation with the Monmouthshire and Glamorganshire Banking Company in 1836, giving Philip leisure to become High Sheriff the following year.

Chapter Nine

Widows inheriting banks from their husbands

West Country, Cornwall: **CORDELIA VIVIAN**, *Helston*; **ELIZABETH MARIA WILLIAMS**, *Redruth*.
Devon: **CHARLOTTE SHORT**, *Exeter*; **REBECCA CANN**, *Exeter*; **LAETITIA DOROTHEA CUMING**, *Ashburton*.
Somerset: **MARIANNE TYNDALL**, *Bristol*; **MARY WAIT**, *Bristol*.

West Country: Cornwall
CORDELIA VIVIAN. Fortune smiled on Cordelia Grylls, one of the more successful banking widows in the West Country. She was born in 1794 into a family of Cornish landowners, settled in the county since the sixteenth century. She was the daughter of Thomas Grylls of Bosahen, the younger son of Richard Gervase Grylls of Helston. Thomas and his wife Mary Millet had three sons, Humphrey Millet, Thomas and Glyn, as well as three daughters. In 1817, Cordelia married John Tippett. In May 1820 John Tippett assumed the name of Vivian, having inherited the estates of Lieutenant Colonel John Vivian of Pencalenick which had been passed on his death in 1817 to his cousin James Vivian Tippett who himself died in 1820. Among the members of this large and prosperous Vivian family were a local baronet, several industrialists, including copper smelters and owners of tin mines, and in 1824 a Vice-Warden of the Stannaries. The copper smelting business linked the Vivians with another Cornish woman banker's family, Elizabeth Carne of Penzance; Joseph Carne and John Vivian being partners in the Hayle copper smelting plant at St Ives Bay in North Cornwall. There were several other Vivian bankers, among them John Vivian (in 1812)

and John Henry Vivian (in 1819) partners at Truro in Lemon & Co. Captain William Vivian, the baronet's younger brother, and Edward Vivian were partners in Kitson, Vivian & Co at Torquay in 1833.

The young couple, part of two solid upper middle class families, gave their eldest son John, born in 1818, a suitable education at Harrow and Trinity Hall, Cambridge. Young John did not go into banking but took Holy Orders and remained in Cornwall as rector of Cardynhan. Many of Cordelia's cousins, the sons of her uncle Richard Gervase (or Gerveys) Grylls, were also in the church, the Grylls clearly enjoying considerable patronage. John made a suitable match with Henrietta Maria, daughter and co-heir of a connection by marriage, William Robinson Hill of Carwythenack. The Helston bank had been opened by Cordelia's father Thomas Grylls in 1788, when he was only twenty-eight, an enterprising young man, practising as an attorney. The business prospered, applying for a licence to issue promissory notes in 1812 and 1813 under the title of the Union Bank. J R Penberthy, another Helston banker, had issued notes in 1809 and 1810. There is no further mention of this banker and it may be that his note issue was absorbed by Thomas Grylls who then took the name of the Union Bank. Grylls' notes continued to circulate and some thirty years later, in 1845, the issue stood at £17,000.

Thomas Grylls' original bank partnership changed and enlarged over the years and by 1812 Thomas had brought in two new partners, Charles Scott and John Borlase, partner in his attorney firm. After Thomas died in 1813 his eldest son Humphrey Millet Grylls, also an attorney, joined the bank, the business of attorneys having been wound up. Humphrey Grylls was senior partner by 1823, bringing in during the next three years John Trevennen, a connection by marriage, as well as his brother-in-law, Cordelia's husband John Vivian. By 1845 Humphrey's youngest brother Glyn was brought into the bank, forming a family partnership very much in the general style of the most successful private country banks. The partnership was once more connected with the law, both Glyn Grylls and John Vivian describing themselves in the 1845 almanac as solicitors and bankers, though another partner, John Kendall, is entered as banker only. Members of the Grylls' family later entered banking in other Cornish towns; Henry and his son William Michell *(sic)* Grylls in the West Cornwall bank at Redruth in 1863 and at Falmouth in 1877, the title having previously been used by Price & Co in 1811.

On the death of her husband in 1854, Cordelia inherited considerable property including his family house at Pencalenick together with the Manors of Moresk, Tucoys and Gavrigan. In addition she inherited his partnership in the family bank at Helston which her father had founded some eighty years earlier and although she was now sixty she continued her work as a banker for some twenty-five years, being no longer burdened at home with over-seeing the care of a young family. She was active as a bank partner evidenced by a number of mortgages which she granted: *Mortgage for £2,766 in 1857 to Charles Grylls of Lanhydrock Parsonage, clerk, and Glynn Grylls of Helston, gent., helling-stone quarry, dwelling house and grist mill, formerly a fulling-mill called Kiggan mill; Mortgage for £12,500 (grant and conveyance) in 1868 to Arthur Prime of Walberton Sussex, Esq., George Thomas Mowbray of Ashby-de-la-Zouch, Leicester, esq. And Thomas Beale Browne of Andoversford, Glos, Esq. property with Tresimple, Trewednass and tithes.* Later in her partnership at the age of eighty-four and in order to increase the curtilage of the Pencalenick estate she had bought in 1878 a piece of land adjacent to Pencalenick, foreshore and riverbed between high and low watermarks, which was part of Kiggan creek from HRH the Prince of Wales.

This involvement contradicts the suggestion by a local historian that Mrs Vivian took no part in the day to day business of the bank but relied on other partners or on salaried managers. As in the other instances in which this absence of involvement has been suggested, it is hard to credit that a woman of property like Mrs Vivian would resign control to other partners, let alone to managers with a far smaller financial stake in the business. An explanation might be the reluctance of male commentators to credit a woman with banking responsibility except in the case of disaster, when blame is all too readily allocated to her, however implausibly.

When Mrs Vivian reached the age of seventy-nine, she took her younger son James E Vivian, a London merchant, into the bank. Six years later the final partnership included, with Cordelia Vivian and her son, her brother Glyn Grylls and John Kendall. The Institute of Bankers quote *Boase* who write that this bank failed for £79,000. He goes on to say that the bank was sold in 1879, after nearly a hundred years of trading, to Bolitho's for fifteen shillings in the pound, Mrs Vivian paying creditors in full. At her death, aged ninety-one in 1885 she left the Vivian house at Pencalenick to her grandson John William Harold Vivian, the child of her elder son John and his wife Henrietta Maria. Before her death Cordelia had the satisfaction of knowing that her house and her bank would both be in safe hands. Bolitho's, originally a private bank at Penzance, had prospered enabling it to take over several other Cornish banks. By 1890 it had formed a joint stock banking company, absorbed in its turn by Barclays Bank in 1905.

ELIZABETH MARIA WILLIAMS. Several years later another Cornish widow, Elizabeth Maria Williams of Redruth was connected through banking with Cordelia Vivian's family. Cordelia was still a partner in the Grylls bank at Helston when her relatives Henry Grylls and his son, William Michell, Falmouth bankers joined John Michael and Michael Henry William to open a bank at Redruth in 1863 as the West Cornwall Bank. Living only eleven miles apart, Cordelia Vivian is very likely to have become acquainted with Elizabeth Maria, John Michael Williams' wife and have had exercised influence on their partnership arrangements some seventeen years later. The formation of private partnership banks in the provinces as late as 1863 showed great self-confidence, for by this date in the history of provincial banking many banks in country towns had ceased to trade as private partnerships, having joined or formed themselves into joint stock banking companies. Against this trend, the Redruth and Falmouth banks continued to operate together as private partnerships until 1877 when they separated officially, though remaining interconnected through overlapping family partnership. Michael Henry Williams continued as partner at Falmouth while his brother John Michael Williams remained at Redruth. When John Michael died in 1880 his widow, Elizabeth Maria, took his partnership in the Redruth bank, which she carried on for four years with a new partner, John Cady, and a manager, William Treweek, until her death in 1884. At this date the bank rejoined the Falmouth partnership of Williams and Grylls, under the name of the West Cornwall Bank. As with Mrs Vivian's Helston bank, this partnership, too, was absorbed by Bolitho's, eventually part of Barclays.

Devon:

CHARLOTTE SHORT. Charlotte Baring may be said without undue exaggeration to have been born with a silver spoon in her mouth, or less figuratively, with some very appropriate genes for a future business woman. She was born in 1763, the daughter of John Baring II who also seemed a child of good fortune. His father, John Baring I, born in 1697, came to England from Bremen as a young man of twenty and was apprenticed to a serge-maker of Holy Trinity parish in Exeter. The pattern of a successful immigrant, he took out British Citizenship papers six years later and in his early thirties, already the owner of a woollen business in Larkbeare, near Exeter, he made an advantageous marriage in 1729 with Elizabeth, daughter of the wealthy Exeter wholesale grocer, John Vowler. The latter took the opportunity offered by the acquisition of an industrious son-in-law to retire to his country house, Bellair.

John and Elizabeth Baring had four sons, John, Thomas, Francis and Charles, three of whom became bankers, and a daughter Elizabeth. Perhaps wishing to keep links with continental Europe, they sent their eldest son John born in 1730, to be educated in Geneva. When her husband died in 1748 Elizabeth vigorously carried on his woollen business at Larkbeare, to such good effect that she had nearly doubled the £40,000 that he had left her to £70,000 at her own death in 1766, less than twenty years later. Her character became so imperious and domineering that she was nervously spoken of as 'Madam' Baring. However, she may have shown a kinder side of her character to her two-year-old granddaughter Charlotte, whose mother Anne, née Parker, died in 1765. The Barings began to acquire property, moving out of the commercial part of the city in 1737, leaving Palace Street by the South Gate for Larkbeare House, in the semi rural parish of St Leonards. In 1755 John Baring II bought Mount Radford, also in the parish of St Leonard's, for the considerable sum of £2,100. The Barings were now thorough-going country people, for their house, standing on a hill opposite the church, was then the only one between the small village of fewer than thirty houses, and the town. The grounds were improved into a park, but business was not forgotten, for a carriage drive was made through the grounds to the town, for speedier access to their business in Exeter. At different dates John Baring invested in other property, buying the manors of Heavitree and Wanford.

The three sons of John Baring I who were involved in banking were John, Francis and Charles John Baring II, Charlotte's father, founded a bank in Exeter, first listed in 1770 as Barings, Lee, Sellon & Green, and another in Plymouth. The partnership in both towns was the same except that Green, the junior partner in Exeter, was replaced at Plymouth by John Tingecombe. Francis, who was academically brilliant, was educated at Winchester and Christ Church, Oxford, where he obtained a double first He opened the London Counting House in a small way, without even a clerk to assist him, and succeeded so well that he received a baronetcy. His son, Thomas George Baring was created Baron Northbrook. Charles Baring, became a partner in the inter-connected London and provincial Baring banks. John was officially senior partner in all the banks but seldom put in an appearance at any of them.

By 1774 the Exeter partners were John and Charles Baring, John Short senior and William Jackson, a local man, the son of an organist. As so often among provincial banks, Barings was strengthened by links with local partnerships through marriage or professional connections. Charlotte's cousin, Jacquetta, daughter of Francis Baring, married Sir Stafford Northcote Bart, founder of the Western Bank in Exeter. Charlotte's aunt Elizabeth's husband John Dunning was an attorney in Ashburton. His partner was Francis Brooking Cumming the husband of Laetitia Dorothy Cuming another West Country woman banker. John Baring II had inherited a considerable part of the Vowler fortune from his mother in 1766 which enabled the Baring family, no longer considered as immigrants, to prosper in banking and enter the established society of the neighbourhood. Charlotte married John Jeffrey Short of Bickham in 1786. He was thirty-three, ten years older than her and a man already known to John Baring for his interests in the fuller's business, allied to the woollen trade. Their marriage was suitable also as the families were already connected through the wealthy Vowlers, John Short senior having married Susanna Vowler. John Jeffrey's brother William, perhaps not without some assistance from the Vowler influence, achieved success in a wider sphere as sub-preceptor to HRH the Princess Charlotte of Wales. His son, another

Thomas Vowler Short, took Holy Orders and rose to be Bishop of St Asaph. The Short family continued their connection with banking, Charlotte's granddaughter Margaret, marrying Charles Arthur Richard Hoare, banker of Fleet Street.

A man with many irons in the fire, John Baring II, Charlotte's father, became a partner in various businesses as well as banking. Perhaps impelled by too early an independence, he seems always to have wanted something new and soon after founding the Exeter bank he decided on a career in politics. He stood for Honiton in the election of 1774 but failing in this attempt, swore never to try again. Changing his mind, however, he was elected in 1776, having disbursed some £25,000 of his inheritance. It may be that the goal, once attained, did not fulfil his expectations for by 1802 his parliamentary career had ended. He may well have been influenced by circumstances at home, for in 1801 his son-in-law John Jeffrey Short died, still under fifty, and John Baring, himself now seventy, brought his daughter Charlotte into the Exeter bank partnership. At thirty-eight she must have seemed to bring youthful energy, comparatively speaking, into a group of elderly partners, including with her father her uncle Charles and her father-in-law John Short senior. Essentially a family concern, the bank nevertheless had in 1790, taken in a younger, more active partner, Charles Collyns.

By the time John Jeffrey Short made his will in 1800 Collyns had become a friend close enough to be named witness to the testator's handwriting. With Collyns' assistance Charlotte undertook the task of keeping the bank in business over the next ten years. The dissolution of the partnership was recorded in the *London Gazette* in 1810 and in the local paper, *Trewman's Flying Post* of 3 January 1811. At the dissolution she and Collyns were partners along with her father, an eighty year-old who had, in spite of his other interests, remained in the Exeter bank ever since he had founded it some forty years earlier. John Jeffrey Short, whose executors were his wife, his brother William and his father-in-law John Baring, had made ample provision from his landed property for his wife and their two sons and three daughters. An affectionate and considerate man, part of his bequest '*to Charlotte my dearest wife*' makes certain that she can retain her '*own*' jewellery and '*all my plate and trinkets watches and all her jewels and ornaments also my furniture linen cellar coals and other stocks of housekeeping all my books, drawings and manuscripts and particularly all papers of my handwriting.'* A separate sheet leaves an annuity on account of the will of his mother to Mrs Ann Bryant as well as one to his butler William Collop. Clearly a man who had always been particular about his appearance, he left a bequest to William Howe *'my hairdresser of Exeter.'* In the last year of his life John Baring found himself in financial difficulties, but was able to sell Mount Radford and his Exeter properties to his cousin Sir Thomas Baring, who later sold the grounds advantageously to a commercial builder. A transaction profitable for Thomas and surely a relief to John to leave no burden of debt to his daughter. Charlotte's elder son John succeeded to Bickham but died unmarried in 1818. Francis Baring Short then succeeded to Bickham and all John's other properties as well as inheriting land in Exminster directly from his father, so becoming a very wealthy man.

Charlotte had the grief of the early death of two of her children John at twenty-eight and her daughter Anne, unmarried, aged twenty-six in 1825. Fortunately Francis and his wife Emily Lane had a son John to succeed at Bickham and meanwhile, no doubt, to delight his grandmother. Charlotte died at Bickham on 20 May 1833, after a not uneventful seventy years.

REBECCA CANN. There was no silver spoon for Rebecca Cann, banker at Exeter, who dismally illustrates the misfortune that could attend a woman catapulted into banking. She was the granddaughter of Francis Moore, gentleman, of South Tawton. Her father, William Moore, was up at Wadham College, Oxford, and received his MA degree in 1751. Three years later he was presented to the living of Spreyton, some five miles from South Tawton. His first child, Francis, named for his grandfather, was born in 1754 at Spreyton. Rebecca was twelve years younger than her brother, born in 1766 and baptised in her father's church in June the following year. Rebecca was only five when her brother Francis, like his father, went up to Oxford, not to Wadham but to Exeter College. After graduating he was presented to the living of Inwardsleigh, some fifteen miles from Spreyton, where he died after a long illness in August 1795, still only in his forties, barely three months after his sister's wedding. Rebecca was still at home, in the usual role of unmarried daughter, when, at the somewhat anxious age of twenty-nine, on 18 May 1795, she married John Cann, son of John Cann of Fuidge Manor, the largest house in the parish. Her husband was much younger than herself, having only just reached his majority, suggesting a possibility that the match was not gladly welcomed by the old squire. Nevertheless, he provided his son and daughter-in-law with South Beer, a small house only half a mile from Fuidge.

If John Cann senior was anxious to secure the succession and worried about the age of the bride, he was eventually reassured. Although John and Rebecca's first child, Mary, was not born until more than three years after the marriage, she was so quickly followed by Elizabeth, Mark and Ponsford that grandfather John, before his death in 1807 at the ripe age of eighty-four, had the satisfaction of knowing that his son would follow him into Fuidge Manor with a nice little family of four, including two sons. The Ponsfords, for whom the second boy was named, from family connection or a wish to please a god-parent, were the most important local family, having been squires of Drewsteignton for some three hundred years. After his father's death John and Rebecca moved into Fuidge, where six more children were born to them. One, little Rebecca, died in infancy and her name was later given to their youngest child, Rebecca Grace, born in 1816. The following year John Cann decided on a business venture, joining John William Williams in the Exeter bank, calling themselves the Devonshire Bank, the name used earlier by Barings Bank. Williams and Cann perhaps hoped the name would imply continuity.

From the start Williams, Cann & Co issued their own notes and within a year opened a branch at Okehampton. John Cann appears to have been the moving spirit in this expansion, for his name is listed first in the bank title there. He was also a member of the committee for another enterprise, the Bude canal, the line from Northlew to Okehampton, in which undertaking he may have been influenced by the presence in the town of William Cann, a builder and ironmonger, perhaps a connection, who could have been useful in the canal construction. The Cann family had carried on their duties as small squires conscientiously, remembering the poor of the parish in bequests and donating bells to the church. Very probably John Cann envisaged banking as an extension of usefulness to his fellow Devonians, subscribing to the contemporary and not unfounded belief that a bank did good by stimulating investment and increasing employment. Unfortunately, no matter how altruistic John Cann's motives, nor how well he might have succeeded had he been able to continue the business for a longer time, sadly, he died in January 1819 leaving to Rebecca the bank partnership, with the ironic hope that she should carry it on for the good of the family. By this time the eldest two daughters were into their twenties, but she still had the care of a string of little ones, the youngest not yet three years old.

The banks at Exeter and Okehampton were soon in difficulties and by 1820 bankruptcy was unavoidable. Although Rebecca inherited a great deal of real estate and other property, as well as the doomed banking business, this was all subject to the demands of the creditors. The Exeter bank premises in Fore Street were sold, the creditors met in 1822 and by 1826 Fuidge Manor too had been sold. The widow survived the financial ruin, but when she died in December of 1846, aged eighty, the value of her bequest of all her real property and effects to her *'unmarried daughters who had never been married'* (being dowerless), was less than £100. Her oldest son Mark was living at that time at South Tawton with his family, but at Rebecca's death it was her youngest son, Abraham, living in Nottingham, who acted as her executor. She was buried in the chancel of St Michael's Spreyton, where she had been baptised and married. Some of the Cann family later managed to regain their stake in the parish, being described in a directory of 1879 as landowners there.

Rebecca's death was announced in the *Gentlemans' Magazine* as *'Relict of John Cann of Fuidge'* but her death certificate registers her as of *'Mount Radford in the parish of St Leonards in the county of Devonshire.'* In an odd way this links the Canns of the second Devonshire Bank with the Barings of the first of that name. The grounds of Mount Radford, the mansion bought by the Barings, had been sold to Messrs Hoopers, local builders, who had developed the site with terraced houses. These were to be exclusively for *'retired officers, clergy and widows of unimpeachable respectability.'* It is pleasantly possible that Rebecca's remaining years were spent in such suitable company.

At the end of the twentieth century the wife of the farmer living at South Beer, Rebecca and John Cann's first home, was a Ponsford, a member of the family who had for so long been squires of Drewsteignton.

Fuidge Manor, however, had become a picturesque, though somewhat dilapidated, pink-washed farmhouse, crowded in upon by sheds which could scarcely be dignified by the name of farm buildings. The Cann family is remembered in the many memorials to them that cover the walls of the old church at Spreyton. The stone commemorating John Cann has the added inscription to the memory of Rebecca '*Relict of the Above, Deeply Lamented.*'

LAETITIA DOROTHEA CUMING. Another widow who was left a bank only to oversee its bankruptcy is Laetitia Dorothea Cuming. Born in Ashburton, Devon, in 1786, she was the daughter of George Winsor of Ashburton and Laetitia Luscombe of Totnes, towns some five miles apart. Laetitia's brother John was a partner in the Ashburton bank by 1821 but other Winsors appear in later nineteenth century census figures as craftsmen in a small way, coach painters, cabinet makers and cordwainers. At the age of twenty-seven Laetitia Winsor married a Totnes solicitor, Francis Brooking Cuming. At their family wedding, Richard James Luscome, curate of Holne officiated and witnesses were John Winsor, Dorothea Popham Luscombe, Susanna Young and Francis Cuming. The Luscombe family had been settled in Devon since the time of Edward I; one branch were settled in Luscombe and in 1740 a John Luscombe, High Sheriff of Devon, bought the manor of Coombe Royal. John's great grandson, John Luscombe Manning, who died in 1831, inherited the estate from his uncle and took the family name of Luscombe.

The Cumings were connected through the Quicke family of Newton St Cyres with two other Devon women bankers, Rebecca Cann and Charlotte Short. In 1814, Frances, daughter of Thomas Cuming Esq, married John Quicke of Newton St Cyres, near Exeter. The Quickes, who had been settled in the county since the sixteenth century, had intermarried at that time with the Shorts, of Bickham, bankers at Exeter. They were later associated with Rebecca Cann's family. Francis Brooking Cuming combined law with banking, becoming a partner with John Winsor, Laetitia's brother, in the Ashburton bank of Browne, Winsor & Cuming by 1821. After a very short time in the bank, Francis died in 1822. His wife was left his partnership in the final few years of the Ashburton bank and its branch at Totnes. The bankruptcy was gazetted in the crisis year of 1825, the partners succeeding in paying six shillings and eight pence in the pound. Laetitia lived on to February 1852. At her death her son Francis Brooking Cuming acted as executor to her will which showed her assets were less than three-hundred pounds.

Presumably there was a family trust, as Mrs Cuming was, in fact, able to leave some valuable property to her son and her daughter. In her will dated 15 June 1843 and a codicil dated 22 November 1847 Laetitia left her large house in Fore Street, Totnes, to her son. This contained a drawing room, a front parlour or dining room, complete with silver and napkins. The bedrooms included Laetitia's own bedroom and dressing room, the front bedroom and dressing room, her son's room, the White bedroom and the Green bedroom, *'other beds performed in the house,'* as well as the servants' back attic. The stables and coach-house were on the other side of the lane called Behind-the-Walls. In the codicil her daughter Laetitia was left the adjoining house and all the furniture. The considerable amount of silver and the books in all the downstairs rooms were to be divided between her son and daughter.

Laetitia's brother John Winsor received five-pounds *'for mourning.'* She remembered those who had served her well, leaving 19 guineas to John Yabbicomb, accountant at Totnes and five pounds to her servant Elizabeth Shellabeare and *'a pension of five pounds a year from the family when she became too old to work.'* Laetitia Dorothea Cuming was undoubtedly meticulous in providing as well as she might for family and servants and it was unfortunate that her talents had no opportunity to show themselves in the Ashburton bank.

Somerset:

MARIANNE TYNDALL. In Bristol two widows, Mrs Tyndall and Mrs Wait, inherited banks within a few years of each other. Marianne Schimmelpenninck married Thomas Tyndall II, a young man of twenty-two, in 1786. He was a third generation banker, his grandfather, Onesipherus Tyndall, a West India merchant and drysalter, having founded the Bristol Old Bank in 1750. Onesipherus continued in the partnership for seven years and was followed into the bank at his death by his son Thomas I. Among early partners were successful business men such as Harford Lloyd, a Quaker and partner in the Bristol Brass

Wire Company. The Tyndall family prospered well enough to build a mansion, known as the Fort, in Bristol's Berkeley Square. Later, the family were obliged to sell it, but succeeded in buying it back in 1798, four years after Thomas Tyndall II joined the bank. This Thomas was active outside banking, becoming Deputy Lieutenant for Gloucestershire and Bristol as well as Colonel of the Bristol Volunteers in 1803.

Though still a young man in his forties, Thomas died in 1804. A deed of that year appointed his widow to '*take his share*' in the bank. Marianne continued as partner until 1809 when their son Thomas reached his majority and joined the Old Bank. He married Mary Sybilla Hill three years later, and retired in 1837, a few years only before his death in 1841. A highly successful concern, the Old Bank continued well past its 1850 centenary, merging in 1891 with their London agents Prescotts, eventually becoming a constituent of the Westminster Bank.

MARY WAIT. Mary Jago was the second Bristol woman banker. Her father John Jago married Olympia Matthews on 16 October 1770 and Mary was born to them on 10 July 1776. The Jago family had long been connected with that of Walter Prideaux, banker at Kingsbridge and through him with other banking families such as Were and Fox. Mary married Daniel Wait, sixteen years older than she in about 1788. Daniel was a younger son of the Waits of Woodborough who had been established there for several generations. He was an active member of the community, becoming Sheriff in 1798 and Mayor in 1805. He was not a member of an old banking family but was one of the founders of the Castle Bank in 1810. Typically of provincial bankers, the partnership between the families of Ricketts, Thorne and George was strengthened by intermarriages.

The bank quickly began to issue its own promissory notes, as did many other banks in Bristol applying for a licence to issue notes in 1812 and 1813. The Waits' address given in the licence application list in 1812 is Stoke Croft though their bank premises were in the Old Dutch House. An eccentric Amsterdam merchant, captivated by three local shop frontages, brought over their three wooden frames in one ship to Bristol at the turn of the century. He set them up on the corner of the

High Street and Wine Street; not inappropriate for a bank with partners in distilling and porter brewing trades. Soon after their arrival in Bristol these premises were occupied by John Vaughan, a goldsmith credited with having been *'the father of Bristol banking'* because his grandson John II added banking to his family goldsmith's business, when he became a co-founder of the Castle Bank in the Old Dutch House. Bristol thus provides one of only two examples in the provinces of the development from the business of a goldsmith into that of a bank, something so often found in London banking.

Daniel Wait died in 1813 only three years after the opening of the Castle Bank. Mary Wait thus succeeded to the comparatively new bank less than a decade after Marianne Tyndall took over the Old Bank in 1804. It may be surmised that Marianne Tyndall's tenure of the Old Bank partnership, though of a few years only, influenced Daniel Wait's decision to appoint his wife to be left in charge of his own fledgling business. Mary retired in 1817, the London Gazette entry for 2 May listing the partners as Jacob Wilcox Ricketts, George Thorne, James George, Mary Wait and John Courtney. They dissolved partnership *'as far as concerns the said Mary Wait.'* She was fortunate that during her time as a banker she could count on much local support, connected as she was through the Jagos with Dartmouth merchants and with several West Country banking families, Fox, Were and Prideaux of Luson, while her Killigrew relations were long settled in the neighbourhood. Neither of Mary's sons became partners in the bank. Her elder son Daniel, born in 1790 took Holy Orders, married Priscilla Thorne whose family were partners in the bank, and settled down as rector of Norton Malreward, where Mary Wait is buried. Her younger son *'William Killigrew Wait Esq of Redlands Lodge, Thornbury, near Bristol'* married in 1826 *'Frances, daughter of Richard Newman Toll of Thornbury Park, Gloucester.'* He thus continued the connection of the family with local landed gentry. The grandson of Mary Wait, Daniel Killigrew Wait settled back near the family business, at Vincent's Hall, Clifton. Daniel and Mary Wait's daughter Catherine married Samuel James; their daughter Catherine Mary married Boddam *(sic)* Castle, a member of a long-established Bristol family.

After Mary retired the Castle Bank continued for another ten years, when one of the managing partners, John Courtenay, became bankrupt, but at the same time, in 1827, the bank merged the business with Stuckey's bank. One of the earliest private banks to take advantage of the legislation which allowed the formation of provincial joint stock banks, Stuckeys Langport bank became a joint stock bank in 1826. They had banks not only in Langport but from 1806 in Bristol and also in Bridgewater. George and Vincent Stuckey were also carriers, operating over a wide network, a powerful and influential concern into which the Castle Bank was absorbed. Stuckeys then removed from their previous home on Broad Quay into the Old Dutch House, where they continued for more than a quarter of a century until it became an ordinary shop in 1855.

Conclusions

An unheralded brief flowering of women's business activity bloomed in the middle of the eighteenth century. Suddenly, women were taking bank partnerships. The enlightened ideas of the eighteenth century may have encouraged parents to expect that their daughters too would enjoy developing their intelligence and skills. Twelve women, sixteen per cent of all women bankers, entered partnerships before 1800 so may have been brought up in these new ideas. Further influences can be seen in the individual connections between women bankers and men of science. The association between Esther Crummer and her husband, bankers at Kington, with James Watt, father and son and Matthew Boulton is one example. The latter also corresponded with Charlotte Matthews, his banker in London. Catherine and John Barker's slitting mills with their consequent interest in the local canal, formed the subject of the detailed and informed correspondence with Erasmus Darwin.

Women entered banking in various ways, the largest number inheriting the partnership from their husbands. It might be considered that these women did not choose to go into banking, but had it thrust upon them. In such instances, however, sensible testators and beneficiaries would undoubtedly have discussed the possibilities, making sure that she was keen to take on the new responsibility. An intelligent, capable wife had plenty of opportunities to impress her husband with the advantages of leaving his cherished concern to her rather than letting it go out of the family into the hands of one of his partners. In this way, and often for long periods, women continued as the senior partner of a bank. Women joined partnerships in other ways. Wives joined their husbands, wives, widows or spinsters joined other relatives. Various combinations of partnerships with relations were made. Two brave women, Ann Butlin and Margaret Campion, founded banks on their own account. (*See* Rugby *and* Whitby)

A woman did not it appears, work on a lower pay scale than a man in the early nineteenth century. In the London bank of Coutts & Co Harriot's earnings were much greater than those of the men partners. Chapter One shows that Harriot Coutts was able to draw far more annually (2007 equivalent of 5.8 million pounds) than any of the male partners of that date. In an indenture of 1811 Sarah Rice retired from the Dover bank of Latham Rice & Co as second partner in favour of her son Edward entering as third partner. Their earnings, appropriate to a country style of living, are in a different scale of magnitude from London. The senior partner drew £1,600 a year and the two junior partners £800 each. Mrs Rice, until her retirement, had presumably drawn some intermediate amount as second partner. That London should have led this innovation and country towns followed seemed appropriate, but less so the background of the first woman banker. It was the marriage of a country girl, Agatha, daughter of Mileson Edgar of the Red House, Suffolk, to Samuel Child, partner in the London bank of Francis Child Esq & Co that led to this innovation. Agatha must have been a remarkable character for after twenty-two years of marriage Samuel took the unprecedented step of leaving her the senior partnership in his bank on his death in 1752. Her tenure proved so successful that she was followed into London banking by a little bevy of women partners. Two members of her own family, her daughter-in-law Sarah and her granddaughter, Sarah Sophia Fane, Countess of Jersey, became partners in Child's bank. The latter died in 1867. After her death the business continued to flourish until in 1924 it was sold, to pay death duties, to Glyn Mills Bank. This in turn was sold in 1939 to the Royal Bank of Scotland. Charlotte Matthews' bank and agency for Matthew Boulton was carried on without fuss from the death of her husband in 1791 until her own death ten years later. Harriott Coutts retained the senior partnership of Coutts bank until her death in 1837. Harriott succeeded in her intention to leave the bank in the hands of Thomas Coutts' descendants, from whom it also became eventually part of the Royal Bank of Scotland. It is tempting to attribute the long and successful careers of Child's and Coutts' Banks in some part to the three highly individual members of the Child family, and the strength of character of that most unorthodox partner, Harriott Coutts.

London did not influence the nearer counties immediately to follow its example for it was in Staffordshire that the first woman entered a country bank partnership. Catherine Barker succeeded her husband, John, in his partnership when he died in 1783. For the next eighteen years she carried on the business of the Lichfield bank and during this time thirteen more women entered banking. Among the country bankers who applied for a licence to issue promissory notes listed in 1812, were fourteen women prepared to accept the added vulnerability. A licence to print money necessitated a strong sense of responsibility. Women partners had ways to prevent a disastrous run on the bank, though not so dramatic as that of their athletic colleague, Jonathan Backhouse of Darlington which were described in the Introduction. Some women succeeded by their calm reaction to danger. In 1834, when Charlotte Ann Eaton had taken over the management of the Stamford bank on the death of her irascible husband she showed her character to be as strong as his but much better controlled. She spoke to a noisy mob of creditors who were demanding the instant repayment of their deposits, outside the Uppingham branch of her bank with quiet, courageous eloquence. Reassured, they returned to their homes, leaving their money in the bank.

A malicious rumour led to a run on the Spilsby branch of Susan Claypon's Boston bank one Saturday in 1874. Mrs Claypon calmly saw to it that the customers who crowded in were served with such promptitude and courtesy that they came back, shame-faced, on the Monday to replace their deposits. Women bank partners came from the same social levels as country bankers in general, that is to say from the comfortably-off middle class, whether in other trades or as landowners. Many women bankers came from long established trading families such as the Dolbys, Sarah Crickitt's parents, successful traders with Portugal. They themselves often carried on other trades as well as banking in common with the generality of country bankers. Margaret Campion of Whitby and Sarah Rice of Dover, for instance, both owned ships in which their trade, Campion to Russia and Rice to continental Europe was carried. With her homing pigeons the latter could also trade in that important commodity, news. Women also pursued more stay-at-home trades; Ann Boulton carried on not only her husband Joseph's bank at Bridgnorth but also his mercer and draper's business. She also shared the proprietorship of the Hampton Iron Lode Company with her bank partner William Bates. Other mine owners included Elizabeth Patton, a Chester banker, who was proprietor of the Flintshire lead mines, and Rebecca Drewry who owned coal mines near her bank in Penrith.

Many country traders carried on their bank in the house of one of the partners, no doubt reducing the strain of going to work. The two houses, numbers 66 and 68 Lymington High Street were occupied as house and bank by Caroline St Barbe in 1881. These are not unlike the tall house in Foregate Street, Chester, where Elizabeth Patton lived. She housed the bank in a basement room with, as the inventory shows, its counters and stools, its desks and chairs and the essential iron chest. Caroline Gunner kept the safe of the Bishop Waltham bank in her cellar, with a rug and table over the trap door. It must have been somewhat of an inconvenience to have to move these morning and evening. By the second decade of the nineteenth century many bankers were aspiring to greater social status through the purchase of land. John Barker, a man of many trades, having bought Harleston Manor from the Egerton family, described himself as a gentleman. Lists of bankers of 1812 and 1813 give addresses of the places where the partners lived; many bankers by then owning larger houses, outside the town and no longer living over the bank in the commercial heart of the city. Nor did the bankers' acquisition of land go unnoticed by the public in general, judging by a comment in *Middlemarch*. Bulstrode, the banker there, is described as '*a speculating fellow with no land*' and the author clearly has no very good opinion of him. Family solidarity proved a useful factor when husband and wife came from families of local squires; such marriages often linking their bank with a number of others in the same or different parts of the country. Charlotte Ann Eaton's family, the Waldies, came from Hendersyde Park, Roxburghshire in Scotland. They had another seat at Kingswood, Northumberland, where they had intermarried with the Ormstons, who were partners in a Newcastle bank. This may have influenced Charlotte's decision to marry a banker, Stephen Eaton of Dene Park near Thrapstone.

Among gentlewomen who took responsibility for a provincial bank on the death of her husband, Leonora Tilden Sampson provides another example, taking charge of the Hastings bank in 1810 when her husband died. Both she and her husband came from ancient local families, her elder brother, George Eversfield, of Catsfield in Sussex, inheriting the baronetcy of Fermor, which had become extinct in the direct line. By an odd coincidence Leonora's husband, John Tilden, also inherited his estate and the name of Sampson from a relative with no direct heir. Apparently 'blue blood' did not at all prevent commercial success, for when Leonora retired, in 1816, she had become a very wealthy woman. Although in general, women country bankers were alike in that they came from a solid middle class, individually they were remarkably diverse. The calm resolution with which some countered a run on the bank was supported by a rather widespread toughness, sometimes ingrained through their upbringing. The Quaker banker, Sarah Darby, was sent off to boarding school at Dr Fells in Worcester with her brothers at the age of eight, though only just recovered from a serious riding accident. She had been crushed beneath the horse which had fallen while a groom had her riding pillion. The firmness of her early upbringing did not result in any outstanding longevity, for after a life time spent in the service of her family, the Dale company and the Coalbrookdale bank, she died at the age of sixty-nine. Many women bankers, however, illustrated their toughness in their longevity, defying the normal life expectancy of their time and holding partnerships for long periods. Twenty remained in their bank for more than fifteen years, four of these for over thirty years. Esther Crummer, for instance, carried on her partnership in the Kington bank for thirty-eight years, as well as taking care of her sick husband. Hannah Grant achieved the distinction of being the oldest woman banker. She was partner in the Leighton Buzzard bank from 1842 until her death in 1853 at the age of ninety-three when she was living with her daughter in Coalbrookdale.

Some women partners indulged themselves in various extravagances, in furnishing their homes, in social pleasures or in dress. In spite of their Quaker simplicity, the Alexanders of Goldrood, Ipswich bankers, and some of the Darbys of Coalbrookdale enjoyed fine furniture, silver and porcelain. The strong-minded Dover banker, Sarah Rice, who had been described as smart as a girl continued to indulge herself in fashionable clothes and furs from London. The Hales of Hambledon, the family of Caroline Gunner, banker at Bishops Waltham, enjoyed parties, cricket and hunting. The Childs, London bankers, also kept a pack of hounds at Osterley Park, their country house. All these bankers, however, earned profits enough for them to take their pleasures without danger to their business. On the other hand, the recklessly extravagant withdrawals from their accounts by the two widows who inherited the Reading bank, was the immediate reason for its failure, though long term, it was attributable to years of inadequate management by their husbands.

A somewhat aberrant frivolity of behaviour was shown by the seventeen-year-old Catherine Maundy, the daughter of respectable timber merchants. Her elopement in 1773 to Gretna Green with the Sandwich banker Samuel Harvey did not prevent her subsequent entry into the bank with him. On the other hand the senior partnership was left on Samuel's death to his cousin Elizabeth, and not to his widow, perhaps an indication of his never quite complete reliance on her steadiness. If so, it would seem something of an injustice for it takes, after all, two to make an elopement.

Very different were the more academic women bankers. Notable among these was Elizabeth, daughter of Joseph Carne, FRS, who shared his geological interests and published her research in learned journals both locally and in London. She also inherited the senior partnership of the Penzance bank at his death in 1858, but did not restrict herself to banking and sciences. This gifted woman also published many books of a philosophical nature, under her own name or a pseudonym. Another who combined banking with literature was Charlotte Ann Eaton. As a girl, she had travelled abroad with her parents and showed her continued interest in continental Europe with two books, one on the battle of Waterloo, the other on the history of Rome, with steel engravings, both of which ran into several editions.

The social conscience of many women partners led them to devote much of their profits on making useful contributions to their community. Rebecca and Anna Sophia Alexander and their family supported a Mechanics Institute and a library in Ipswich. Elizabeth Evans, the Derby banker, built a church in her village and in practical consideration for the health of the girls working in her Darley paper mills supplied them with woollen cloaks and blankets in the winter. Their charitable works were often in education, sometimes for girls in particular. The schools established in Leighton Buzzard by Hannah Grant, with her husband and other Quakers on the Joseph Lancaster system, educated girls as well as boys. In Ipswich Rebecca and Anna Sophia Alexander promoted schools for girls. In Chertsey in 1810 Elizabeth la Coste, too, was active in the cause of women's advancement, supporting the Female Friendly Society there. Darley village also benefited from the school set up by Elizabeth Evans, whose belief in education for girls is clear from her sending her daughter Bessie to the school kept by the Misses Parker, the natural daughters of Erasmus Darwin. Elizabeth Carne, among her many activities, used her money to found schools in many villages nearby, as well as in Penzance itself. Many country people, especially women, must have been grateful for such of the 'three Rs' as they acquired due to these public-spirited women bankers.

The diversity of women bankers is further illustrated in the variety of their religious affiliations; for though the generality attended and often are commemorated in their parish church, Wesleyans, Presbyterians and members of independent churches joined bank partnerships. The eight Quaker women bankers, Rebecca and Anna Sophia Alexander, Sarah, Rebecca and Hannah Darby, Catherine and Catherine Payton Fox and Hannah Grant, form a special group of around ten per cent of women bankers. Another feature of the Quaker women partners derives from the Quakers' frequent intermarriage. The marriage of Hannah, daughter of Hannah Grant, Quaker banker at Hitchin, with Abraham Darby of Coalbrookdale, connected her with the women partners in that bank. Another Quaker, Caroline Payton Fox was related to ten other banking families. Acquaintance between women bankers was sometimes through business ties, Elizabeth Carne and Cordelia Vivian for instance, through partnership between their families in the Hayle copper smelting plant. Other connections were reached through propinquity, as between Jane St Aubyn and Catherine Fox and her daughter, who lived within six miles of each other. Such aggregations, though perhaps gently encouraging, fell far short of being in any way a professional association that could provide real support. The fact that a married woman was legally unable to own any property, even her current earnings, must have appeared an insuperable obstacle to her entering a partnership. One way to avoid the restriction lay in the terms of a marriage settlement entitling a wife to retain her own property and earnings. Thomas Coutts made such a settlement on Harriott when they married.

To achieve their independence, married women had to struggle against further difficulties, domestic and social. Over a period during which young ladies were expected to make the most eligible match they could and be content with their domestic role, it cannot have been possible for them to add the responsibilities for a bank without remark. At the very least they would have risked raised eyebrows and a prodigious amount of gossip in the town. More importantly, the usual lot of women at that time in having large families could not be avoided. Well-to-do women undoubtedly employed nannies and nursery maids to alleviate the burden of rearing their offspring. Ann Boulton and Rebecca Cann each had ten children and Mary Jones thirteen, and though these are the extreme every woman banker with a family had to endure the disorders of pregnancy and the distress of childbirth at rather frequent intervals. Concentration on business matters can have been no easier then to combine with a family than it is today. At that time, as today, a working woman's children had to be brought up largely through intermediaries. Then, governesses and tutors, today minders and day nurseries. Very often their daughters and sons grew up responsible and hard-working enough to carry on the bank successfully. There were exceptions; Margaret Campion's son Robert through his ambition to be accepted as a fashionable gentleman, with his failure to curb his son's extravagance eventually brought down the Whitby bank.

Sarah Crickitt's Chelmsford bank fell to a similar fate. Her son secured unjustified overdrafts at the Ipswich, Colchester and Chelmsford banks, in all of which his mother was a partner. The two at Colchester and Ipswich managed to absorb the loss and weather the economic crisis of 1825 but the Chelmsford bank succumbed. The failure, in which Sarah was directly involved, must have been very much the more disturbing to her from the knowledge that the unthinking greed of her son was in large part responsible for it and the consequent misery to the neighbourhood. Happily, these two failures are balanced by the history of two other banks in the same towns. Mary Richardson, Margaret Campion's youngest sister, partner in another Whitby bank, must have been alarmed when she saw the foolish behaviour of her nephew after her sister's death in 1804. Mary was spared the knowledge of the disaster, for she died in 1840, a year before her nephew failed. Her trust in her own son Christopher's capacity as a banker was justified in the event, for after entering the partnership on her death in 1840, he took the bank successfully through the next six years to amalgamation with the York City and County joint stock banking company.

The Crickitt's Ipswich banking and political rivals, the Alexanders, also provides reassuring evidence of a working mother's successful children. Rebecca's eldest son John Biddle Alexander, joined the bank alongside his mother in 1838 and continued until the year before his death in 1863. Her second and third sons, George and Frederick, joined the bank when she retired in 1845, George in Ipswich and Frederick at Woodbridge, where he took charge of their branch. The latter retired in 1882 and died the following year, when his obituary, recording his possession of the virtues typical of a Quaker banker, noted that '*he was scrupulously just and conscientious.*' This private partnership bank was so firmly established that it continued on its long career until absorption into Barclays Bank in 1896. The toughness and resilience of women bankers would seem to have gained the respect of contemporaries in one instance at least.

Though social decorum may have been breached, contemporary authors refrained from poking fun at the new bankers. On the contrary, the popular Victorian novelist, Mrs Oliphant, for instance, allows two women to show their skill in banking, presenting them as more efficient and responsible than their male colleagues. Her plot describes the country bank set up by Mr Vernon in the small town of Redbridge and the prosperity enjoyed by town and bank under the founding partner. His son manages only to keep what has been gained, while John, the grandson could not achieve even that level of competence. Without business sense or recognition that '*a country banker has all the money of the district in his hands*' John indulged his own and his wife's extravagance. When a crash became unavoidable, John then made off for France, leaving the bank to its fate. Cousin Catherine, who had kept her mother's legacy in the Redbridge branch of the Bank of England, now used her own money to rescue Vernon's bank and carried it on with the same success as her grandfather had done. Later John's daughter, Hester, the eponymous heroine of the novel, coming back from France to join her aunt in Redbridge, proves equally effective. Mrs Oliphant concludes that '*It is the fashion of our time that women should understand business and be ready for any emergency.'* The fulminations against woman's intelligence (cf *pp. xiii and 97*) by the egregious tutor in George Eliot's 1860 *Mill on the Floss*, is replaced here in 1883 by a much more favourable view.

The performance of women in banking over the intervening period had no doubt exerted its influence on public opinion. All three London banks with a woman in the partnership either closed without loss or continued for many years until eventual absorption into banking companies. Women country bankers did less well. Eight out of the fifty-eight country banks failed while a woman was still in partnership. This fourteen per cent failure rate compares remarkably well with the thirty per cent failure rate of all country bankers. No defence against failure was found in the circumstances or character of the women bankers.

A comparison with another minority group, the Quakers, may offer a suggestion. Like women, Quakers, were also restricted in access to university education and professions. Caroline Fox, in response to Elizabeth Carne's question as to how Quakers, with their belief in simple living, made so much money in banking, was categorical. *'Industry, perseverance and energy have been habitually cultivated by them.'* She concluded that as the money market is the only outlet permitted to their energies *'they were apt to succeed therein.'* The same qualities, essential to a woman combining work with family responsibilities, may explain how women, as the figures show, were apt to succeed. The achievements of the women considered here, in the light of the obstacles that had to be overcome, provide evidence of a successful, if short, struggle for the right to work. Enlightened ideas may have influenced the education of this group of women, but no suggestion appeared of any support from feminism.

Ten women had entered bank partnerships before the publication in 1792 of Mary Wollstonecraft's *Vindication of the Rights of Women* (cf *p. 97*). The first, Agatha Child, forty years before this date. The three members of her family in the bank naturally knew of the activities of the others. The last, Lady Jersey and her contemporary, the Duchess of St Albans, can hardly have avoided knowing of the other's London banking activity. Within such families as the Darbys and the Alexanders family partnerships were known to each other of course. A woman partner in a bank applying for a licence to issue notes would have seen, when she looked at the 1812 lists, that it included fourteen women. Apart from such instances, however, each of these very diverse women may well have believed herself to be making her solitary way in the world of business. No evidence was found that women bank partners took heart from the growth of the feminist movement, nor does it appear that any knowledge of the women in banking had percolated through to the activists. Each woman banker, assuming her own right to work, made her own way along the road to professional gender equality.

References

Where *"Country Banks"* is given as a reference, this includes the references listed in the Select Bibliography in Volume One of that publication.

ALEXANDER ANNA SOPHIA
Cornforth Country Life 1986 Alexander.
Bidwell W H *Annals of an East Anglian Bank, Norwich*; Agas Goose 1900.

AMPHLETT CHRISTIANA MARIA
Personal communication
Atkins Mrs K, Archivist, Dudley Metropolitan Borough 1989.

BARKER CATHERINE
King Hele, *Desmond Erasmus Darwin Letters* ed. CUP 1981 Bolton.
Personal communication
Hughes Miss Megan, Principal Area Librarian, Staffordshire County Council 1987.
Peck Joanne, Staffordshire & Stoke-on-Trent Archive Services 2001.

BEDWELL OLIVE
Godding John, *Norman's History of Cheltenham* Longman Green 1863.
Personal communication
Parker Graham, Liberal Studies Dept, Gloucester quoting unpublished work 'Banking in Gloucestershire' compiled by T Hannan-Clark 1992.

BENN MARIA
Personal communication
Whitney J L S, *Rugby Advertiser* July 1961 on the opening of the Benn Memorial Hall.
(This reference applies also to **BEDWELL**)

BOULTON ANN
Dickinson Henry William, *Matthew Boulton* CUP 1937.
Personal communication
Carr Anthony, Local Studies Librarian, Shropshire County Council 1988.

BRADLEY ELIZABETH
Boys William F A S, *Collections for a History of Sandwich, Kent* 1792.
Personal communication
Deighton Elizabeth, 1998.

BUTLIN ANN
Rugby Advertiser July 7, 1961.
Personal communication
Whitney J L S with *Rugby Advertiser* 1991.

BUTLIN CATHERINE
Country Banks

CAMPION MARGARET
Barker Rosalind, *Prisoners of the Czar* Highgate Publications 1992.
Browne H B, *Chapters of Whitby History* 1946.
Burke's Landed Gentry Vol III under Archer.
Hardcastle Daniel, *Banks and Bankers* Whitakers 1842.
Sykes Joseph, *The Amalgamation Movement in English Banking* 1826 to 1926, London 1926.
Personal communication
Browne H B, Whitby Museum 1991: Jones Dr.S, *Maritime History of the Port of Whitby* 1700 to 1914, doctoral thesis and chapters of *Whitby History* (with chapters *Early Whitby Banking Houses*: W A Oldfield) A Brown & Sons Ltd Hull & London 1946.

Denier Mrs Anne, Whitby 2008.
Ellis Mr J, Midland Bank Manager Whitby 1991.

CANN REBECCA
Burke's Landed Gentry Vol. 1.
Cary's New Itineraries 1817
Dymond Robert D S A, *History of the Suburban Parish of St.Leonard's Exeter* 1873.
Foster Joseph, *Alumni Oxoniens,* OUP 1891.
Polwhele Revd Richard, *History of Devon* Vol II 1793.
Ryton John, *Banks and Bank Notes of Exeter* pr pr c/o National Westminster Bank 1984.
Worthy Charles, *History of the Suburbs of Exeter* Exeter 1892.
Worthy Charles, *Devonshire Will* Exeter 1896.
Personal communication
Napier Revd C J L, Rector of Drewsteignton 1989.
Rowe Mrs M, County Archivist, Exeter 1989.

CARNE ELIZABETH
Boase G C, *Bibliotheca Cornubiensis* 1874 & 1882 *Collectiana Cornubiensis* 1890.
Dictionary of National Biography Pub 2007.
Cornish Telegraph Obituary, 10 September 1893.

CHILD AGATHA AND SARAH
Ashby J F, *The Story of the Banks* Hutchinson 1934; chapter 1; chapter 5.
Burke's Peerage 1883; Earls of Jersey and of Westmorland.
Clarke Phillip, *The First House in the City* London 1973; *Child & Co 1673 to 1973.*
Countryman July 05, Tortworth Chestnut, Sarah Child.
Earl of Jersey's MSS Footnote 50 (Historical MSS. Commission. Appendix to 8th Report, p. 100a.) from: *Lincoln's Inn Fields: Nos 39 to 43 (Royal College of Surgeons), Survey of London*: volume 3: St Giles-in-the-Fields, pt 1: Lincoln's Inn Fields (1912), pp. 48–58.
Hardcastle Daniel, *Banks and Bankers* Whitakers 1842.
Harris Eileen, *Guide to Osterley Park* 1994.

Hilton Price F G, *A Handbook of London Bankers* Leadenhall Press London 1890–1.

Personal communication

Stertley Park Learning Centre Visitors' Booklet 2004.

West Alison, Ipswich County Record Office 2006.

CLAYPON SUSAN

Davis S M, *Banking in Boston, History of Boston* Series No. 25, 1976.

Porter Herbert, *Lincolnshire Magazine* vols I to II September 1932 to July 1938.

Personal communication

Hopkins J and Mather Toni, Boston Library 1988.

COUTTS HARRIOT

Ayling Stanley *A Portrait of Sheridan* Constable London 1985.

Baron-Wilson Mrs Cornwell, *Memoir of Harriot Duchess of St Albans* preface by Margaret Baron-Wilson Henry Colburn, London 1839.

Harris Margaret, *Memoirs of Harriot Mellon, Duchess of St Albans* Remington 1863.

Healey Edna, *Coutts & Co 1692-1992 The Portrait of a Private Bank* Hodder and Stoughton 1992.

Healey Edna, *Lady Unknown. A Life of Angela Burdett-Coutts.* Pickwick & Jackson London 1978.

Price F D Hilton, *A Handbook of London Bankers* Leadenhall Press London 1890–91. *passim.*

Smith John Guthrie and Mitchell John Oswald, *The Old Country Houses of Old Glasgow Gentry* (1879).

Stokes Veronica, *A Bank in Four Centuries* pr pr Bemrose Security Printing, Derby 1982.

Personal Communication

Emerson Stuart, The Heraldry Society of Scotland 2006.

Long Isabel, Assistant Archivist, Coutts & Co.

Moir-Sharpe Priscilla, 2006.

Peters D D J, Archivist, Coutts Bank 440 The Strand London.

The Court of the Lord Lyon, Edinburgh 2006.

COBB ELIZABETH

Personal communication

Bond D R, Archivist Northamptonshire Records; Kettering Public Library 1989.

Fuller John, Pemple Baptist Church Records 1990.

Gotch Christopher, 1990.

Scouse Mrs. June, Kettering Parish Records 1990.

COX CHARLOTTE

Sayers R S, *Lloyds Bank in the History of English Banking* 1957.

Personal communication

Bensusan Butt J, Branch Archivist, Essex 1988.

Coverley P R J, Branch Archivist, Colchester and North Essex Stanwell House, Colchester.

Dancy Jane, Local Studies Librarian, Colchester 1988.

CRICKITT SARAH

Colchester Central Register of Baptisms in the Dutch Church at Colchester. Publications of the Huguenot Society of London vol xii 1905.

Marsh C M, *Life of the Revd William Marsh* 1867.

Miller-Christie, *A History of Banks & Banking in Essex* reprinted from the Journal of the Institute of Bankers 1906.

Oxley-Parker Lt. Col J, *Early History of Colchester Banks* Essex Review Vol.61 1852.

Personal communication

Bensusan Butt J, Branch, Archivist Essex 1988.

Coverley T R J, Branch, Archivist Colchester and North Essex Stanwell House, Colchester 1994.

Dancy Jane, Librarian Essex County Council, Colchester.

Smith Janet, Principal Archivist Essex Record Office, Chelmsford 1988.

CRUMMER ESTHER

Banks R A, *Guide to Hergist Croft* 1988.

Country Banks

Personal communication

Banks Mr W L, 2003.

Fenn Dr Roy, Personal Archivist to W L Banks 2000.
Oliver R C B, 1988.
Ross Dr John, photographs 2001.
Sinclair J B & Fenn R W D, *The Border Janus* 1995.

Cuming Laetitia Dorothea
Personal communication
Smith Miss L, Librarian Ashburton quotes P J Bottrill, Exeter Trewman's *Flying Post*.

Darbys Hannah, Rebecca, Sarah
Labouchere Rachel, *Abiah Darby* Sessions York 1988.
Raistricht A, *Dynasty of Ironfounders* Longmans 1953.
Trinder Barry, *The Darbys of Coalbrookdale* Phillimore 1974.

Deane Lucy
Country Banks
Le Fay Deirdre, *Jane Austen; A Family Record* by William Austen-Leigh and Richard Arthur Austen-Leigh revised and enlarged British Library 1990.
Personal communication
Corley T A B, Faculty of Letters and Social Sciences, Reading University 1975.
Smith Margaret, Senior Librarian Local Studies Group, Reading 1990.

Doorne Eleanor Mary
Country Banks
Personal communication
Woollacott Kate, Heritage Office, Kent County Council Libraries.

Dowden Ann
Alton Official Guide, Local Authority Publishing Co. consulted 1996.
Country Banks
Personal communication
Cross T, Curator of Curtis Museum, Alton Hants 1994.
HH Judge McLellan E B, 1990.

DREWRY REBECCA
Country Banks
London Gazette 1836 page 3128.
Hardcastle Daniel, *British Losses by Banking Failures 1820-1857* Waterlow 1858.
Personal communication
Cunningham Helen, Research Officer, Carlyle 1996 quotes *Cumbrian Directory* 1847.
Smith Miss M, Librarian, Penrith Library 1991.

EATON CHARLOTTE ANN
Country Banks
Hodgson R A, *Gunners Bank* Part 1, Vol. III 1977.
Hodgson R A, *Gunners Bank* Part 2, 1978.
Porter H, *Lincolnshire Magazine* Vol. III page 169.
Portsmouth Archives Review Vol. II.
Personal communication
Gunner R A, 1979.

EVANS AND MIDDLEMORE
London Gazette 1816 page 30.
Notts Journal 23 September 1802.
Personal communication
Brown Joyce, Librarian, Grantham 1991.
Crute Mr B, Librarian, Mansfield 1991.
Kingscott Judy, Nottingham Librarian, photocopy *Philimore's County Pedigrees Notts.* Vol. I 1991.

EVANS ELIZABETH
Coleridge Samuel Taylor Letters edited E L Griggs, Clarendon Press 1956.
Estlin John Prior, Unpublished letters from Samuel Taylor Coleridge to the Rev. John Prior.
Personal communication
Haigh Bernard, Central Derby Librarian, photocopy Derby Evening Telegraph 25 July 1980 *Story of Elizabeth Evans.*
Glover S, Derby County Librarian *History of the County of Derby* Mosley Derby 1829, two volumes.

Bibliographical Notes (by Tilley) on Thomas Evans, William Evans & Walter Evans.

FANE, SARAH SOPHIA (*SEE* CHILD)

FOWLER SARAH
Personal communication
Braddock Catherine, Leek Librarian 1990. Photocopy of part of the Fowler family tree taken from *Miller Old Leeke* volume 1 1891.

FOX, CATHERINE AND CATHERINE PAYTON
Barclay Fox's Journal edited by R L Brett Bell and Hyman 1979.
Burke Landed Gentry 1847 Volume 1.
Charles, William and Philip Fox & Bond Peter, *History of G C Fox & Co. Falmouth* 1987.
Fitzmaurice R M, *British Banks and Banking*.
Nym Horace, (editor) *Caroline Fox of Penjerrick Memories of Old Friends*.
Personal communication
R M Fitmaurice 1988.
Springell Kim Redruth, photocopied pages from '*Old Falmouth.*' Susan E Gay 1903 quoting Wilson Lloyd Fox.

GRANT HANNAH
Brown Maureen and Masters June, *The Bassetts; Leighton Buzzard's First Family* published by Leighton Buzzard's Research Group 1998.
Willis R B, *The Coming of a Town The Story of Leighton Buzzard and Linslade* written and published by R B Willis 1873 and 1984.
Personal communication
Lee Inglis Anabel, Librarian, Leighton Buzzard Library, photocopies from book out of print: *Leighton Buzzard Past and Present Year Book* 1905.

GUNNER CAROLINE
Personal communication
Gunner R H, June 1990.
HH Judge McLellan E B, Hambledon 1990.

HARVEY FRANCES ELIZABETH
Personal communication
Kennedy Jean, County Archivist, Norfolk Record Office – no reference to Elizabeth Harvey found in Norfolk sources.

HARVEY KATHERINE
Burke's Landed Gentry under Dyne of Gore Court.
Country Banks
Personal communication
Deighton Mrs Elizabeth, Sandwich 1998.

HASLEHURST HANNAH
Country Banks

HOWARD ANN
Country Banks

JONES MARY
Country Banks
Twiggs 1930 Directory

LA COSTE ELIZABETH
Country Banks
Personal communication
Mackenzie Beryl, Runnymeade Borough Council 1988 quoting 1851 census records.
Mirylees Duncan, Surrey Local Studies Library 1988.

LUTENER ELIZABETH
Country Banks

MARRATT GRACE
Country Banks
Personal communication
Bensusan Butt J, Branch Archivist, Essex 1988.
Coverley P R J, Branch Archivist, Essex County Council 1988.

Chattisham Mrs Marjorie Betton, Ipswich 1990.
Dancy Jane, Local Studies Librarian, Colchester, 1988.

MARSH CATHERINE
Country Banks
Personal communication
Corley T A B, University of Reading, Berks 1995 quotes *The Earliest Reading Bank, Marsh, Deane & Co. 1788–1815 Archaeological Journal* Vol 66.

MARTEN ELIZABETH
Country Banks
Personal communication
James Lynne, Area Librarian, Dyffwd County Council 1988.

MASSEY MARY
Country Banks

MATTHEWS CHARLOTTE
Uglow Jenny, *The Lunar Men* Faber and Faber 2002.

MIDDLEMORE SUSANNA – SEE EVANS AND MIDDLEMORE.

MORRIS JANE
Country Banks
Personal Communication
Nixon Janet, Surrey County Council, Guildford Library.

MUSGRAVE ELIZABETH
Country Banks
Personal communication
Lavis Clare, Somerset County Council 1992.

PATTON ELIZABETH
Country Banks
Personal communication

Green Mrs E M, Research Consultant, Cheshire Record Office 1996.
Hays Dafydd, Gwernymynydd Flint 2000.

RICE SARAH
Country Banks
Burke's Landed Gentry page 706 under Rice. Isaac Lefroy Fellow of All Souls, Rector of Ash and Compton Surrey (*sic*).
Le Fay Deirdre, *Jane Austen; A Family Record* by William Austen-Leigh and Richard Arthur Austen-Leigh revised and enlarged. British Library 1990.
Personal communication
Hammond Margaret, Cambridge 1989.
Peters Mrs B J, Archivist Coutts Bank.
Rice Brian, *Lives of the Rices of Dane Court; the story of a landed family* chapters 2, 3, 14, 16 and appendix 2 Maberley Phillips 2006.
Rice Henry Esq, quotes *Dover Directory* circa 1790 and *The Mariners Mirror* 1956/9 volume 42 to 45, 1987.

RICHARDSON MARY
Personal communication
Barker Mrs Rose, Whitby 1991.
Ellis J, 1991 (*see under* **CAMPION**).
Turner Sandra, Assistant County Librarian, Whitby Branch Library 1991.

RIMINGTON MARY
Burkes Landed Gentry
Country Banks
Crick & Wadsworth: A Hundred Years of Joint Stock Banking Hodder & Stoughton, 1936.

ROUND MARGARET
Marsh Revd D, Life of the Revd William Marsh D D 1867.
Personal communication
Coverley D R, Branch Archivist, Colchester North Essex Stanwell House Colchester 1988.

RUNDLE ELIZABETH
Country Banks

ST AUBYN JANE
Burke's Landed Gentry.
Personal communication
Cryer Rev G D, Plymouth 1997.
Elliott J R, Area Librarian, West Devon Plymouth 1989.
Goord Revd Martin, Torrington 1998.

ST BARBE CAROLINE MARY
Country Banks
Personal communication
Ryder Jackie, Reference Librarian, Hampshire County Council 1991.

SAMPSON LEONORA TILDEN
Country Banks
Personal communication
Bourke Judith Kinnison, Herstmonceaux, East Sussex 1997.
Davey C R, East Sussex County Council 1988.
Haine Pamela, Team Librarian, Local Studies East Sussex Hastings Central Library 1988.

SHORT CHARLOTTE
Burke's Landed Gentry, 1947.
Country Banks
Dymond Robert, *History of the Suburban Parish of St. Leonard's Exeter* 1973.
Hoskins W G, *Industry, Trade & People in Exeter* University Press Manchester 1935.
Mallet Bernard, *Thomas George, Earl of Northbrook* London 1906.
Newton Robert, *Eighteenth Century Exeter University of Exeter 1984.*
Oliver George, *Biographies of Exonians* reprinted from *Flying Post* 1849–1850.
Ryton John, *Banks & Banknotes of Exeter* Professor pr pr c/o National Westminster Bank 1984.
Worthy, Charles *History of Suburbs of Exeter* 1892.

Zielger Philip, *The Sixth Great Power Barings 1760–1929* Collins 1988.
Personal communication
Orbell Dr M J, Archivist, Barings 1988.
Rowe Mrs, County Archivist, Exeter 1988.

SIMMONDS MARY
Country Banks
Personal communication
Essex Louise, Librarian, Nuneaton Library 1997.
Goord Revd Martin, Torrington, 1998.
Oglesby Miss L, Team Librarian, Coalville Library Leics. 1988.
Raftery Michael, Team Librarian, Leicestershire Libraries 1988.

SKEY SARAH
Browne E O & Burton J R *Short Biographies of the Worthies of Worcestershire Worcester 1916.*
Burton J B, *History of Bewdley* London 1883.
Wedley Isaac, *Bewdley & Its Surroundings* Kidderminster 1904.
Gentleman's Magazine 1810.
Radio Times May 2003 re. BBC 2 'Secret Lives of the Artists.'
Personal communication
Gladdon George, Bewdley Public Library 2001.

SMITH ANN FAWTHORPE
Country Banks
National Archive on-line Register – Newby, Robson & Cadle Solicitors Stockton 1818.
Royal Canadian Institute Proceedings of the Society of Antiquaries in Newcastle-upon-Tyne Vol. IX 1919–1920 ed. Robert Blair.
Personal communication
Reference Librarian, Stockton Reference Library, Stockton-on-Tees 1992.

SWAINE HANNAH
Country Banks
Cudworth W, *Rambles Round Horton* Bradford 1886.
Roth H Ling, *The Genesis of Banking in Halifax* King (Halifax) 1914.
Personal communication

Betteridge Dr R, Calderdale District Archivist 1988.

TYNDALL MARIANNE

Cave C A, *A History of Banking in Bristol* Crofton Hermonns 1899.
Life of Mary Anne Schimmelpenninck London 1858.
Personal communication
Dyer Miss S, Bristol Central Library 2002.

VIVIAN CORDELIA

Fitzmaurice R M, *British Banks and Banking* D Bradford Barton Ltd 1975.
Vivian J L, *The Visitations of Cornwall* Exeter 1887.
Personal communication
Fitzmaurice R M, 1988.
Spence Alison, Archivist, Cornwall Record Office 2009.

WAIT MARY

Burke's Landed Gentry 1847
Cave C A, *A History of Banking in Bristol* 1899.
Country Banks
Personal communication
Dyer Miss D, Bristol Central Library 2002.

WILKINSON ANN

Country Banks

WILLIAMS ELIZABETH MARIA

Country Banks

WOOTTEN-WOOTTEN SARAH

Jackson's Oxford Journal Dec. 1850.
Matthews P W & Tuke A W History of Barclays Bank Ltd. *(p. 276) Pub 1926.*
Oxfordshire Record Office Ref: B15/3 and Ref. 15/3/2D/10.
Personal communication
Jenkins Stephanie, Oxford 2009 website 'History of Headington'.

General

Ardener Shirley and Burman Sandra ed. *Money go Round* Berg Oxford/Washington 1995.

Ashmolean Museum, University of Oxford 2010.

Dawes Margaret and Ward-Perkins C N, Country Banks of England and Wales, The Chartered Institute of Bankers 2000.

Effinghan Wilson, 1894. (General and Child)

Paterson's Roads 1826.

Perkins Dudley, Tradesmen's Tokens II.

TABLE INDICATING THE FATES OF THE WOMEN BANKER'S

Key to the Fates: J=Joint stock. SF=Subsequently failed. C=Closed. F=Failed.

SURNAME	FIRST NAME	START	END	PARTNERSHIP	FATE
ALEXANDER	Rebecca	1838	1845	Alexander & Cornwell	J
ALEXANDER	Anna Sophia	1863	1878	Alexander & Cornwell	J
AMPHLETT	Christiana (Jan-Dec)	1801	1801	Dixon & Co	J
BARKER	Catherine	1781	1803	Barker & Co	SF
BEDWELL	Olive	1790	1792	Bedwell & Co	C
BENN nee BUTLIN	Maria	1846	1868	A.Butlin & Son	C
BOULTON	Ann	1796	1803	Boulton & Bates	SF
BRADLEY	Elizabeth Catherine	1810	1815	Harvey & Co	J
BUTLIN	Ann	1791	1829	A.Butlin & Son	C
BUTLIN	Catherine	1846	1868	A.Butlin & Son	C
CAMPION	Margaret	1800	1804	Campion & Co	SF
CANN	Rebecca	1819	1826	Williams, Cann & Co	F
CARNE	Elizabeth	1858	1873	Thomas Batten & Co	J
CHILD	Sarah	1782	1793	Child & Co	J
CHILD	Agatha	1752	1763	Child & Co	J
CLAYPON	Susanna	1859	1881	Garfit & Co	J
COBB	Elizabeth	1802	1806	Cobb & Co	SF
COUTTS	Harriott	1822	1837	Coutts & Co	J
COX	Charlotte	1845	1893	Bridges & Co	F
CRICKITT	Sarah	1803	1825	Crickett & Co	F
CRUMMER	Esther	1821	1857	Cheese & Co	J
CUMING	Laetitia Dorothea	1822	1825	Browne & Co	F
DARBY	Rebecca	1810	1836	Darby & Co	J
DARBY	Sarah	1810	1836	Darby & Co	J
DARBY	Hannah	1810	1836	Darby & Co	J
DEANE	Lucy	1805	1815	Marsh & Co	F
DOORNE	Eleanor Mary	1811	1864	Day & Co	J
DOWDEN	Ann	1790	1797	Baverstock & Dowden	C
DREWRY	Rebecca	1834	1840	Rebecca Drewry	F
EATON	Charlotte Ann	1834	1859	Jackson & Co	J
EVANS	Elizabeth	1796	1808	Evans & Co	J
EVANS	Ann	1816	1871	Moore & Co	J
EVANS	Catherine Ann	1816	1871	Moore & Co	J
EVANS	Charlotte Dorothy	1816	1871	Moore & Co	J

EVANS	Dorothy	1816	1871	Moore & Co	J
FANE	Sarah Sophia	1806	1867	Child & Co	J
FOWLER	Sarah	1829	1846	Fowler & Co	SF
FOX	Catherine	1812	1823	Fox & Co	C
FOX	Catherine Payton	1812	1823	Fox & Co	C
GRANT	Hannah	1842	1853	Bassett & Co	J
GUNNER	Caroline	1872	1906	Fox, Gunner & Co	J
HARVEY	Frances Elizabeth	1795	1812	Day & Co	SF
HARVEY	Catherine	1813	1815	Harvey & Co	J
HASLEHURST	Hannah	un-known	1784	Haslehurst & Co	F
HOWARD	Ann	1812	1817	Howard & Co	SF
JONES	Mary	1828	1836	Sir R Salusbury	J
LA COSTE	Elizabeth	1846	1851	LaCoste & Co	C
LUTENER	Elizabeth	1829	1841	Price & Co	SF
MARRATT	Grace	1812	1815	Mills & Co	C
MARSH	Catherine(Lady)	1805	1815	Marsh & Co	F
MARTEN	Elizabeth	1810	1814	Marten & Co	SF
MASSEY	Mary	1812	1888	Gales & Co	SF
MATTHEWS	Charlotte	1791	1801	Matthews & Co	C
MIDDLEM-ORE	Susanna	1816	un-known	Moore & Co	J
MORRIS	Jane	1810	1812	Coggan Morris & Co	SF
MUSGRAVE	Elizabeth	1812	1827	Musgrave	SF
PATTON	Elizabeth	1790	1803	Thomas Patton	C
RICE	Sarah	1797	1811	Latham & Co	SF
RICHARD-SON	Mary	1825	1840	Clarke & Co	J
RIMINGTON	Mary	1830	1843	Rimington & Co	J
ROUND	Margaret	1857	1886	Crickett & Co	J
RUNDLE	Elizabeth	1810	1818	Gill & Co	J
SAMPSON	Leonora Tilden	1813	1816	Tilden & Co	SF
SHORT	Charlotte	1801	1810	Barings & Co	C
SIMMONDS	Mary	1810	1831	Fisher & Co	SF
SKEY	Sarah	1806	1824	Skey & Co	C
SMITH	Ann	1816	1816	Elston & Co	F
ST AUBYN	Jane	1810	1818	Nelson & Co	SF
St BARBE	Caroline Mary	1879	1896	St Barbe & Co	J
SWAINE	Hannah	1803	1807	Swaine & Co	C
TYNDALL	Marianne	1804	1809	Tyndall & Co	J
VIVIAN	Cordelia	1854	1879	Grylls & Co	C

WAIT	Mary	1813	1817	Ricketts & Co	C
WILKINSON	Ann	1810	1814	J. Wilkinson	C
WILLIAMS	Elizabeth Maria	1880	1884	Williams,Grylls	J
WOOTTON WOOTTON	Sarah	1887	1904	Wootten's Bank	J

Index

A

Alexander, Anna Sophia 79, 87, 88, 144, 145
Alexander, Rebecca 79, 85, 86, 87, 144, 145
Amphlett, Christiana Maria 35, 36, 37, 38, 48, 54

B

Barker, Catherine 101, 116, 117, 141
Bedwell, Olive 21
Benn, Maria 17, 18
Boulton, Ann 101, 113, 114, 141, 146
Bradley, Elizabeth 35, 44, 45
Butlin, Ann 17, 18, 140
Butlin, Catherine 17

C

Campion, Margaret 17, 18, 19, 20, 53, 99, 140, 141, 146
Cann, Rebecca 123, 130, 131, 132, 133, 146
Carne, Elizabeth 35, 40, 50, 51, 52, 53, 54, 123, 144, 145, 148
Child, Agatha 55, 57, 58, 140, 148
Child, Sarah 1, 2, 3, 4
Claypon, Susan 79, 90, 91, 141
Cobb, Elizabeth Mary Warner 101, 110, 111
Coutts, Harriot 1, 4, 5, 6, 7, 8, 11, 12, 13, 14, 15, 70, 140, 145
Cox, Charlotte 79, 81, 84

Crickitt, Sarah 79, 80, 81, 82, 141, 146
Crummer, Esther 101, 104, 106, 107, 108, 139, 143
Cuming, Laetitia Dorothea 123, 128, 133, 134

D

Darby, Hannah 21, 24, 26, 29, 33, 48, 103, 104, 145
Darby, Rebecca 21, 24, 25, 26, 48, 143, 145, 148
Darby, Sarah 21, 22, 23, 24, 25, 145
Dean, Lucy 55, 59, 60, 61, 62
Doorne, Eleanor Mary 55, 75
Dowden, Ann 55, 62
Drewry, Rebecca 21, 26, 27, 142

E

Eaton, Charlotte Ann 79, 88, 89, 90, 141, 142, 144
Evans, Ann Elizabeth 36, 101, 111, 112
Evans, Catherine Ann 101, 111, 112
Evans, Charlotte Dorothy 101, 111, 112
Evans, Dorothy 101, 111, 112
Evans, Elizabeth 29, 30, 31, 32, 36, 47, 48, 144, 145

F

Fane, Sarah Sophia 1, 2, 3, 4, 140
Fowler, Sarah 101, 117, 118
Fox, Catherine 35, 47, 48, 49, 145

Fox, Catherine Payton 35, 39, 49, 50, 54, 145

G

Grant, Hannah 26, 101, 102, 104, 143, 144, 145
Grove, Sarah 58, 59
Gunner, Caroline 55, 63, 64, 65, 66, 142, 143

H

Harvey, Frances Elizabeth 45, 79, 92
Harvey, Katherine 35, 44, 45
Haslehurst, Hannah 21, 159, 168
Howard, Ann 35, 47

J

Jones, Mary 101, 121, 146

L

La Coste, Elizabeth 75, 76, 145
Lutener, Elizabeth 29, 34

M

Marratt, Grace 79, 84
Marsh, Catherine 55, 59, 60, 61, 62
Marten, Elizabeth 101, 119, 120, 121
Massey, Mary 29, 33
Matthews, Charlotte 55, 58, 139, 140
Middlemore, Susanna 101, 111, 112
Morris, Jane 29, 33
Musgrave, Elizabeth 29, 33

P

Patton, Elizabeth 1, 93, 94, 95, 96, 97, 98, 142

R

Rice, Sarah 53, 55, 67, 68, 69, 70, 71, 72, 73, 74, 75, 140, 141, 143
Richardson, Mary 18, 93, 99, 146

Rimington, Mary 93, 99, 100
Round, Margaret 79, 82, 83, 84
Rundle, Elizabeth 35, 41, 42

S

St Aubyn, Jane 35, 39, 40, 41, 145
St Barbe, Caroline Mary 55, 66, 67, 142
Sampson, Leonora Tilden 55, 76, 77, 142, 143
Short, Charlotte 123, 127, 128, 129, 130, 133
Simmonds, Mary 35, 42, 43
Skey, Sarah 101, 115, 116
Smith, Ann Fawthorpe 29, 33, 34
Swaine, Hannah 35, 38

T

Tyndall, Marianne 50, 123, 134, 135, 136

V

Vivian, Cordelia 123, 124, 125, 126, 145

W

Wait, Mary 123, 124, 134, 135, 136
Wilkinson, Ann 101, 118, 121
Williams, Elizabeth Maria 123, 126
Wootten-Wootten, Sarah 101, 112, 113

172